From Sprites to Dark Horses

(A Girlguiding Journey)

Avril Stouse

First published 2010

Reprinted January 2020

Dedicated to my Mother

Hilda

her Granddaughter Karyn

and her

Great Granddaughters

Abiee and Louisa,

to mark the

Centenary Year of Girlguidng

2010

'If it isn't fun,
it isn't guiding'

Spirit of Guiding

Tune: 'Streets of Laredo'

1. Today we remember our sisters in Guiding
   Living in countries so near yet so far.
   And as we remember, we ask God to bless them,
   Guide them and lead them wherever they are.

2. Today I'm a Brownie, thinking of others,
   Tomorrow a Girl Guide I know I shall be.
   But I'll still remember my Law and my Promise,
   And the spirit of Guiding will grow up in me.

3. Today I'm a Girl Guide, working for others.
   Tomorrow I hope I will work for them too.
   For we are all sisters in this world Guiding Movement,
   Learning and loving in all that we do

4. Today I'm a Ranger, living for service,
   Using my gifts for community needs.
   Knowing and giving, my life is worth living,
   Rangering forth I will go where life leads.

5. *Today a Lieutenant, learning whilst leading,
   And Rangering onwards for service and fun –
   All the time knowing that the great game of Guiding is
   Encouraging Guiders and girls – everyone.

6. *Today I'm a Guider, teaching and leading,
   Trusting with faith in the work that I do.
   Knowing and sharing, and hoping that always
   The spirit of Guiding will spread the world through.

7. *Today a Commissioner, leading, supporting
   The girls and their Guiders in all that they do.
   Whatever the challenge, decision or outcome,
   I'll never forget I'm a Guide through and through.

8. *Today an Adviser, helping our leaders
   Provide for our girls in that great Guiding way.
   Embracing new trends and initiatives gladly –
   Upholding that vision of times far away.

9   *Today I'm a Trainer, enthusing our members,
Enhancing their skill for 'our girls in the lead'.
I'm sharing my passion for Guiding with others, and
Steering them forward, whatever their need.

10   *And now I am President of Sussex West County.
An honour and privilege – yet humbling task.
Supporting our members, promoting and sharing
My passion for Guiding – what more could I ask.

11   *Today I'm in Trefoil, loving each moment,
Supporting, promoting our great Guiding game.
I've noticed the changes since I've been a member but
The spirit of Guiding remains just the same.

*extra verses written to fit my story

From **Sprites** to **Dark Horses**

Chapter One

'Today I'm a Brownie thinking of others'

My Journey Begins

'The Iron Room', in Plumstead, was where it all began.

This was in 1949, just four years after the end of the Second World War. My locality was still littered with bomb sites which had once been dwellings. Now these sites were magnets for us children – ruts and slopes to run up and down and wild flowers in abundance to pick – with no hint of the dangers that may be lurking.

At the end of our road, around the corner and up the hill, was the Brownie Meeting place. The Iron Room was situated in a tiny wooded triangle at the junction of Cantwell Road, where I lived, and Eglinton Hill in Plumstead, South East London. This corrugated iron construction seemingly comprised of just one reasonable sized room. I remember neither toilets nor a kitchen but maybe I had no need to use these facilities so they were of no consequence to me.

As soon as I became seven, my mother took me along to my first meeting. I cannot remember much about those early days but I do recollect later wearing my most professionally sewn home-made brown uniform for the first time. Mum had been a Court Dressmaker and had made clothes for the Princesses Elizabeth and Margaret so I was used to wearing expertly made dresses and my Brownie uniform was no exception. The material for my Brownie dress and my brown beret, yellow neckerchief and leather belt were all purchased from the Guide Shop in Victoria.

No doubt I was a little nervous when it came to the moment when I had to 'make my Promise' as a Brownie – quite a nerve-racking experience for a shy and very reticent seven year old. However, I passed my first test, was enrolled and was soon embarking on my Guiding journey.

'I promise on my honour
To do my duty to God and the King.
To help other people at all times
And to keep the Brownie Law'

I'm on my way

So, I was a real Brownie and, in 1949, I began my wonderful and fulfilling journey through Guiding, one which has been so immensely fulfilling and rewarding.

My pack was the 5th West Woolwich, attached to All Saint's Church, Shooters Hill. There was another pack, 1st West Woolwich, also attached to All Saint's, and we met up at our monthly Church Parade Services.

I remember only my Brownie Leaders being at Church Parade so it would seem that there were too many Brownies for one pack and so they ran two.

Brown Owl was always the last to arrive for Church Parade. We met on the corner of our road and she always arrived just in time, whilst wiping from her 'battle dress' (as Guider's jackets were then called) the remains of her bacon and egg breakfast. Her ample bosom seemed to attract the dripping egg!

All Saint's Church had suffered bomb damage and was soon considered unsafe for services. Church Parades were later held in the nearby Mission Hall in Herbert Road and this became the temporary church for many years until the original bomb-damaged church was knocked down and eventually rebuilt.

An early memory of a Brownie meeting in 'The Iron Room' was a gathering of more than just our Brownie Pack and we sang:

> *'Star of the evening,*
> *Pretty little evening star.*
> *Star of the evening,*
> *Shining on the cookhouse door.'*

After each rendition of this chorus, a six was selected to sing a nursery rhyme. No repetition was allowed and so sixes were eliminated when they couldn't think of a different rhyme to sing in the tie allowed for thought. Maybe this gathering was an early version of Brownie Reels and it obviously sowed the seed for my later love of Campfire Singing.

The Club Room

We didn't seem to stay in 'The Iron Room' for long as our meetings moved down the hill to 'The Club Room' which was situated between the Vicarage and the Church. Maybe the 'Club Room' had been bomb damaged too and we had moved back once repairs had been made. This must have been the church hall.

I have rather more memories of Brownie meetings in 'The Club Room' and can vividly picture members of each six holding hands in a line, with the Sixer at the front, and skipping round the toadstool singing,

> *'We're the Brownies, here our aim –*
> *Lend a hand and play the game.'*

We would then face inwards and hold out first our right hand, then our left and finally both hands whilst reciting.

'Lend a little with your right hand,
Lend a little with your left hand,
Lend a little with both hands,
LAH, LAH, LAH.'

It took me a while to realise that LAH, LAH, LAH wasn't just singing 'lah', but a 'Lend a Hand' LAH!

I was eventually a very proud Sixer of the Sprites, leading my six around the toadstool and singing with gusto.

'Here we are the sprightly Sprites
Brave and helpful like the knights'

I took my Brownie responsibilities VERY seriously and always made sure that my Promise badge was sparkling, my belt polished, my tie immaculately folded with a perfect knot, my dress ironed and spotless, my shoes well polished and my brushed beret perfectly placed upon my head.

It was soon after I became a Brownie that I discovered my school teacher, Miss Johnson, was a Brown Owl. Sadly, we never discussed Guiding or Brownies in school but we were allowed to wear our uniforms on Thinking Day. Miss Johnson wore hers too and that was when the discovery was made.

Not long after my first Thinking Day at school, I attended a Jamboree - for Guides, Scouts, Cubs and Brownies – at the Co-op Woods in Abbey Wood. I was to return to the Co-op Woods 60 years later, with our baby caravan, to stay on the Caravan Club Touring Site, the Caravan Club having purchased the woods many years before my return visit.

What a time I had with my Brownie friends at the Jamboree but I fear we made rather a nuisance of ourselves, as we found Miss Johnson and continually pestered her throughout the day!

No Pack Holidays for us

I was never to experience the joys of Pack Holidays as a Brownie, maybe because we were a London Brownie Pack and facilities were limited, or because of the recent war and money was needed for much needed repairs and renovations to property. However, I do remember meeting at the end of Herbert Road one day, dressed in my brown tunic, wearing sandals on my feet and carrying my haversack with precious picnic inside.

We clambered into the back of a soft topped delivery van that had benches along each side. There seemed none of the safety rules and regulations of later years. Where we went, I do not know, neither do I remember what we did when we arrived at our destination. I just remember the joy and pleasure of climbing into a vehicle with anticipation of a ride in something other than a red London number 53 bus! Our Mothers waved us off and I'm sure we must have had a wonderful day. I wonder where we went or what we did.

Another challenge for me

Until the 1970s, Brownies and Guides were 'enrolled' as members of the Guiding Movement when they made their Promise. This terminology was used as their names were not officially recorded on registers (the roll) until they made their Promise. Even today, you hear members of all ages talk about enrolment ceremonies instead of the correct. 'Promise Ceremonies'.

Once I was enrolled, the correct terminology for 1949, I began to work on my Brownie Second Class Test. This was soon after renamed 'The Golden Bar'.

I thrived on the challenge of working towards the next stage of my Guiding journey, achieving my 'Golden Bar' and another badge for my Mother to sew on my uniform. I hadn't yet reached the stage of sewing on my own.

I drew and coloured the composite flags of the Union Jack, loved the skipping clause, always had string in my pocket to tie the knots, practiced balancing a ball on a board for posture, learned the health rhyme, had no trouble with the sewing clauses or the rules of the road but really, really struggled with keeping my finger nails well cut and clean. I was a nail biter and this was so, so hard.

B-P once made up a rhyme to give Brownies an easy way of remembering how to keep fit. I remember learning this but was not totally sure what it meant until later.

'Only feed on wholesome fare,
Through your nostrils breathe fresh air.
Clean yourselves inside and out,
Twist and bend and run about'.

Greater responsibilities

When I passed my Golden Bar Test, I was already the Second of the Sprites and had collected my first service star, having been enrolled for at least a year. It was a real thrill to have my Golden Bar Badge presented to me along with my Sixer stripes. Wow, I was now the Sixer of the Sprites and I just thrived on the responsibility.

Outside Brownies I was always quiet, shy and very diffident but the whole ethos of Brownies seemed to instill in me the confidence to try new things and not worry if I didn't at first succeed. Being a Brownie meant I could 'try, try and try again' without feeling threatened and thinking that I was going to be shouted at for not getting things right, as frequently happened at my school. It was developing my leadership skills, though I obviously wasn't aware of this then.

So, I was a Sixer. I took great pride in preparing my Six for Brownie ring, making sure that each member was smart and standing straight before we danced around the toadstool to sing our special rhyme. I loved helping my Six learn and understand the meaning of the Promise, Law and Motto and I really enjoyed being able to present a new recruit to Brown Owl so that she could be 'enrolled'. Sometimes, as Sixers, we were given the opportunity to organize games. This was very special.

Yet another meeting place

It was at this time that our weekly meetings moved to another hall. The Club Room was soon to be demolished along with our lovely, though bomb damaged, church. All Saint's Church was to be rebuilt on the site of the original and the Club Room site was to be sold to Woolwich Borough Council for new flats.

An obsolete hall had been purchased by the church in Dallin Road, the end of which was opposite the site of the old Iron Room. So, all three halls were the same distance from my home. This new hall was really modern, clean and smart, with two meeting rooms, though one considerably smaller than the other. It also had a modern kitchen and cloakrooms. We said goodbye to the spiders, cracks and grime and thoroughly enjoyed our new premises, complete with storage.

It was from this hall that I began working towards my 'Brownie First Class Test' or 'Golden Hand Badge'. As far as I am aware, no other Brownies in our pack had achieved this and so I worked and worked on trying to perfect all the requirements.

This badge was an enormous challenge for me as it meant that, when I was ready to be tested, I had to travel to the dockyard area of Woolwich and be tested by people unknown to me. My confidence had grown at Brownies but would I cope in a strange and different environment? Time would tell.

I enjoyed learning semaphore, but would I remember enough to pass on the day of the test? Learning and reciting poems was an everyday occurrence at school so learning two verses of the National Anthem was no problem, and I was even happy to sing them.

The gardening clause was another matter altogether. What a challenge! Still, to this day, I have trouble keeping any kind of plant alive. However, I somehow managed to grow a hyacinth – such a relief.

I had already discovered the fun of tying knots and enjoyed working fancy knots on cord, so knots were a doddle. The knitting, too, was little of a challenge as I had knitted from a very early age, being able to read patterns and knit fancy clothes for Rosebud, my baby doll.

I remember practicing fire lighting at home but, during this time, our open fire was removed and replaced by an all-night boiler and I definitely was not allowed to interfere with that. So, I practiced washing and ironing my Brownie tie instead.

My mother was very nervous of me using a kettle. I was allowed to fill it, as then it was cold, but as soon as the water boiled on the hob and the kettle became hot, my mother would get very agitated and that would make me nervous. However, Mum stood back, which must have been very hard, and allowed me to make the tea. How palatable it was, I know not, because I have never liked drinking tea.

Now the skipping was great fun. I just loved skipping and could actually skip over one hundred 'bumps' (a double turn of the rope) without stopping. It was a favourite pastime of mine, along with playing two or three balls up the wall or doing handstands. I would spend ages upside down with my feet up the wall and my dress tucked in my knickers so it didn't cover my face.

If two balls or hand stands had been on the syllabus, I would have passed with flying colours. However, the ball clause was overarm throwing and I found this really difficult. Indeed, when it came to the test, we had just one ball with several Brownies needing to use it. My turn came to throw and the ball went sailing over a high wall, never to be retrieved! Oh dear. Not only had I ruined my chances, but I had also prevented the others from completing the ball clause too.

Fortunately, I was given another chance and allowed to return the following week to try again. This was when I realiised that being a Brownie was so much better than being at school as, at Brownies, I wasn't shouted at or belittled.

My rice pudding, which I had to take to the test, was really creamy and tasty – not like the tinned rice pudding of today. What a joy it was to scrape round the dish and prise off the soft crust which came off in little brown curls.

I remember practicing how to deal with clothing on fire and had great fun, in the Dallin Road Hall, rolling younger Brownies along the floor wrapped in their coats. What a blessing that our new hall was so clean, otherwise there would have been several irate mothers complaining of dirty Brownie clothes.

The big day came

So, the time came for me to take the test. Mum came with me and helped me carry my hyacinth, rice pudding and knitted navy scarf (navy so I could use it for Guides). The venue was quite a distance from where we lived, I believe in the Dockyard area of Woolwich and I remember a hall, for the 'inside' clauses and a road, for the outside ones. How different today, with such busy traffic. No Brownies would ever be allowed to play on a busy city road, let alone use one for testing purposes.

The test took two evenings, as I had to return for the ball throwing clause, as you will remember. However, I passed and was elated. I skipped to the bus and then all the way home. We called into the 'Club Room' on the way. This had not yet been demolished and several Guide Leaders were having a meeting. They all seemed to know where I had been and offered me congratulations when they heard of my achievement. I was ecstatic.

It was with great pride that I sewed on my Golden Hand Badge. Yes, I had moved on to another phase of Guiding – that of sewing on my own badges. Fortunately, I seemed to have inherited my mother's needlework skills.

Sad news and a Coronation

In February 1952, King George VI died and the country was in mourning. All members of the Guide Association wore black arm bands on their sleeves as a sign of respect. I remember my black armband though cannot remember on which arm it was sewn.

Then, there was great excitement as plans for the Coronation were put in place. Our new Queen Elizabeth II had been a Guide and a Ranger and so we all felt that she was really special as she belonged to our Guiding family.

There was to be a 'Coronation Tribute', a challenge for each Guiding member, and a special badge worn once we had carried out this tribute. Our pack's tribute was tidying up the small garden outside our hall and planting bulbs.

It was very difficult to remember to change the wording of our Promise. No longer could we 'do our duty to the King', nor could we sing, 'God save our gracious King'.

Time to move on

During Coronation Year, in 1953, I reached my 11th birthday and so it was time to move on to Guides. My mother had already taken me to the Guide Shop, at CHQ in Buckingham Palace Road, to buy my Guide Uniform as my birthday present. I was so excited.

My last meeting also coincided with the last ever meeting of the 5th West Woolwich Brownie Pack. I knew that, once I had left, my Brownie Pack was going to close and become a Girls' Brigade Company. Midway through this last meeting, two Commissioners arrived, resplendent in their white shirts and cockaded hats. They seemed very austere and rather frightening and they certainly didn't help the discomfort I was experiencing by wearing my new Guide uniform. Mum suggested I wore it, so no choice really.

I felt I shouldn't be at the Brownie meeting as I was dressed as a Guide and, for some reason, I refused to sit down with my Six when we were working with one of the Brownie Leaders. I think I thought I ought to look like a Guide Helper and stand behind the Brownies. What an embarrassment.

So, my time as a Brownie was over. What a wonderful start to my Guiding journey and I'm so grateful that my Brownie Leaders waited until I was due to 'fly up' to Guides before they closed the pack. I could wear my Brownie wings on my Guide Uniform – my first badge!

My brother was a Scout several miles away at Wesley Hall on Plumstead Common. This Methodist Church had a thriving Guide company and so it was decided that I would join the Wesley Hall Guides.

It was just before Christmas of 1953 that I became a member of the 6th Plumstead Common Girl Guides.

'Tomorrow a Girl Guide I know I shall be.'

Chapter Two

'Today I'm a Girl Guide working for others'

The new recruit

So many Guides and a cacophony of sound met me as I entered the hall behind Wesley Hall Methodist Church in Timbercroft Lane. I was quite a way from my home and knew there would be no others from my school. However, being a Brownie had given me the confidence to enter the meeting place on my own and I was confronted with a bubbling two-toned sea of blue blouses and skirts with splashes of green ties as Guides rushed to and fro before the meeting began.

Captain and Lefty greeted me, as I entered, and they made me feel so welcome. I was placed in the hands of Marion, my Patrol Leader. She seemed so grown up and organised and I was soon sitting in my Patrol corner and being introduced to the other Bantams. So now I was a Guide, albeit a recruit, and wondered what adventures were in store for me.

I heard a shrill whistle, a long blast, followed by instant silence. This was already a very different start to the one experienced at the beginning of a Brownie meeting. More whistling, three short blasts followed by a long one (Leaders fall in), and Marion left us to stand in front of Captain alongside the other Patrol Leaders. They marched in a spaced out line behind each other and were soon joined by the members of their patrols. I was shown where to stand and I was quickly to learn that this was Roll Call followed by inspection.

I felt really smart in my Guide uniform and much more comfortable than the first occasion I had dressed as a Guide, on my last evening as a Brownie. My blue shirt was neatly pressed and waiting for the various badges I hoped I would soon be stitching on the pockets, sleeve and shoulders to join my Brownie wings (earned as a 'First Class' Brownie) and my Coronation Tribute badge. My green tie was starched and folded with knot neatly tied at the top, making it the correct length of three fingers from my belt. A reef knot at the back of my neck under the collar, secured it in place. I was used to tying a reef knot behind my back as I had practised this as a Brownie. Wearing my uniform to my very first Guide meeting was such a thrill and I felt so proud when Captain told me how smart I looked. I even seemed to have impressed her with my reef knotted tie. What excitement and anticipation.

That first evening seemed to fly by and in no time at all we were singing 'Taps' and then time for home. Mum was waiting outside for me for our long journey home. Her concern was that I wouldn't wake up in time for school the next morning. Nine o'clock was way after my bedtime and we still had to travel home. Maybe I was feeling tired but I certainly wasn't going to admit it! I could hardly wait a week for the next meeting. It had just been great and I had started my journey as a Guide.

Three weeks on and in at the deep end!

My first few weeks as a Guide were spent getting to know the other Guides whilst preparing for a mini Gang Show that Wesley Hall Guiding and Scouting members were performing together, just three weeks after my first meeting.

Being a 'newby', I hadn't expected to take part but how wrong I was. I soon discovered that I was to participate in a sketch and sing the many songs we were singing with the Scouts, Cubs and Brownies. Talk about being thrown in at the deep end but it was such fun and a wonderful way to experience the friendship that Guiding and Scouting offers.

As a Brownie, I had only met other Brownies when taking part in activities but here was a whole new experience – a seemingly huge family of Guides, Brownies, Cubs, Scouts and leaders, and all so friendly. I knew that I was going to enjoy myself.

I don't remember the songs we sang but I can vividly picture the Brownies dressed up in 'pretty dresses' with huge blobs on their cheeks They sang, 'The Wedding of the Painted Doll'. Another performer was Jean, a Ranger, who sang 'Golden Earrings' and her dangling golden earrings seemed to dance at the end of her earlobes as she sang. What a voice – I was so impressed.

My big moment came towards the end of the show. I was dressed as an urchin in clothes borrowed from my brother – grey shorts and a shirt that was far too big for me. I had to smudge my face with shoe polish to complete the impression. What the plot was I do not know but I had the 'punch line'.

I walked on to the stage at the beginning of the sketch with other members of the cast and just had to stand there throughout, holding a slice of bread and jam. After much dialogue – goodness knows the content – I had to shout, 'and there's your bread and jam', whilst rubbing the offending slice in the face of another 'boy urchin'. This was my first big moment as a Guide and a wonderful start to my many happy years at Wesley Hall.

Working together

The Gang Show had been the start of so many occasions when the Guides and Scouts worked together. Our joint activities always finished with a good old 'sing song'. Stan, the Scout Leader, led the campfire singing, whether inside or out. If outside, we had a real fire and inside a very authentic pretend fire of logs, red and orange paper and, of course, the light bulb to give it a glow. The songs we sang we were very Scout orientated, as I discovered when I later joined in Guide only Camp-fires. Nevertheless, they were such fun and we always went home very hoarse from singing so lustily.

There was a flourishing Parents Committee that worked tirelessly to ensure that both groups had the necessary financial support. Many joint functions were held and the support was tremendous. Dad, for a time, was the chairman and, during his term of office, he organised 'Shows' where children and adults submitted crafts, cooking, produce etc, in the hope that they would win a certificate or two. These were always well supported and it was such fun and not a problem if we weren't given a certificate after all our efforts. Our items could usually be used to pass some clauses in our Guide tests.

So, now I was a Guide

Our Gang Show completed the Autumn term of 1953 so we had a few weeks holiday before starting our meetings again in January 1954. Once back after Christmas, I began in earnest to prepare for my 'Tenderfoot Test' in order to make my Promise as a Guide.

I had already completed the first clause – that of attending Guide meetings regularly for a month. I now had to recite the Promise, motto and laws to Lefty to prove that I knew them. I had been learning the laws at home during the Christmas holidays, convinced that I would never remember them. Mum, however, came to the rescue as she taught me the 'Law Rhyme'. That was such a help.

'Trusted, loyal, helpful.
Sisterly, courteous, kind.
Obedient, smiling, thrifty.
Pure in body and mind.'

Despite being wintertime, we went down to Plumstead Common to practice our tracking skills and so that part of the test was quickly ticked off. We used the whistle and hand signals every week, so another tick. I had learned a little about the Union Flag whilst a Brownie, so it didn't take long to add to my knowledge in order to gain the necessary tick for clause 5.

My Guide pocket always carried the requisite length of string for knot tying. I just loved tying knots, maybe as my fingers were nimble and dextrous, having sewed from a very early age. Marion taught me how to whip the end of a rope and I was soon able to prove this to Lefty so that another clause was completed.

As we had no bed at Guides, Mum had to send a letter to Lefty to say that I could strip and make a bed. I was nearly there – just learning about the origins of the Guide movement and the meaning of the Guide and World Badges stood between me being a Tenderfoot and becoming a member of the great Guide family.

My Enrolment Ceremony was soon upon me. Excitement was tinged with anxiousness as I wondered if I would remember what I had to say and do. Maybe I would forget to salute in the right place or forget my Promise or what my honour meant. Would I 'freeze' in front of Captain who seemed a little daunting to me then. I hadn't really got to know her as Lefty had been in charge of the Tenderfoots.

Mum arrived for the Ceremony. The Colour Party had a practice and then 'it began'. Wow. Marion presented me to Captain, and soon it was all over. I had remembered what my honour meant, I had made my Promise, Captain had pinned my Guide Badge on my tie. I had saluted Captain, the Union flag and the Company flag, and I had been presented to the Guide Company. **I was a Guide.**

Fun, Fun, Fun

I just loved being a Guide and I looked forward so much to our weekly Monday meetings. I liked the structure of the meetings – a game to begin, followed by Patrol time, roll call and inspection, the 'work' and learning new things but in a fun way. More games after that, then Taps and home.

I quickly made new friends, especially when a group of Brownies 'flew up' to Guides in the second week after Christmas. Because my Brownie Pack closed down and we had no Guides attached, I had not experienced this ceremony – though I did earn my wings as a First Class Brownie.

Amongst this group of Brownies was Ann, from my infant reception class, who was to remain my Guide friend throughout. Sadly, she didn't join me as a Ranger in future years but we are still in touch as I write. Captain and Lefty were Ann's aunts and her parents were both very involved with the Scouts. Another of Ann's aunts was Brown Owl, so a true Guiding and Scouting family.

My first Guide hike

It was tradition in the 6th Plumstead Common Guides to go on a hike every Good Friday. We would take the red London buses to Farningham, in Kent – the end of the 'red bus line' – and make our way to Wrotham on a green country bus. Once at Wrotham, Captain would give us our instructions and we would follow the Ordnance Survey Map to the point chosen by her for each Patrol to cook lunch on open fires.

Mum had ensured, on this first occasion, that I was 'kitted out' correctly with sensible footwear, haversack and waterproofs, along with some spending money and, of course, the requisite number of sausages. I suppose there hadn't been many occasions when I had been away from my parents for a whole day, so quite an adventure.

I remember being so impressed with my Patrol Leader, Marion, as she demonstrated how to turf and lay the fire. I'm not sure that we managed to light the fire with just two matches and Captain probably had to come to our rescue to keep it going, but it was such fun cooking our sausages, potatoes and beans, with banana fritters for 'pud'.

Although we lived in a fairly open area of London with parks and commons close to home and our meeting hall, it was just wonderful to get out into the real countryside and walk along the sides of recently sown fields or skirt fields of cows or sheep and soak up the glorious views and country air. It was quite magical.

Once the hike was over, we began, during our meetings, to prepare for camp. We always had a weekend camp at Whitsuntide, followed by a week's camp in the summer. There was great anticipation for this very first camp.

The joys of camping

At our Guide meetings, we practiced tying up our bedding rolls, brushed up our knot tying, learnt how to do square lashing ready for the gadgets for bedding rolls, wash stands and plate racks – not forgetting the 'welly rack'.

My first ever camp was at Cudham, the Guide site in Kent. I was allowed to leave school early as we were leaving Wesley Hall at 4.00pm. My school and house were at least a half hour's brisk walk away from Guides. School didn't finish until 4.00pm so it was exciting to be allowed out of school. I don't think my current teacher, Miss Fisher, approved but my old teacher, Miss Johnson, still taught the younger children so I knew I would have her approval. You can read about Miss Fisher in my book, 'One More Step'. As it was, Mr Phillbrick, the Headmaster, was the one who had given permission.

We were all at Wesley Hall at the appointed time and the camping gear was loaded on the furniture removal van above the driver's cab. We Guides then piled in and found space to sit amongst and on the hessian latrine screens. Such an adventure, more so, maybe, because my usual mode of transport was a London tram or bus, sometimes a train and more usually 'shank's pony'.

Our mothers waved us off and we were away. Once out of the built up area, the singing began and we changed our waving to passers by to actions to complement the songs. My repertoire was growing – and we sang all those songs that Guiders try so hard to discourage.

Singing and laughter saw the journey fly by and soon we were pulling off the road and bumping along the track to the field. Thankfully, it was still light and dry so our efforts at erecting our bell tents weren't hampered by darkness or rain.

It must have taken quite a time to 'make camp' as no sooner had we moved in to our tent than the whistle signal announced that supper was ready.

Lefty was QM and had set up the altar fire as soon as we had arrived, so we were soon sitting in our horseshoe on our sitters with plate bags at the ready, wondering what was on the menu. I don't remember what we ate but it was good fun not treading on 'the grass table' whilst we went to be served in Patrol order.

Washing up followed and I quickly learned that hot water was always on offer at camp, from a dustbin permanently on the central fire with a 'dibber' to scoop out the almost boiling water. In years to come, I always enjoyed making the patrol washing up stand from branches we saved from camp to camp, until they were too brittle to use. A combination of knots and square lashing soon produced a stand for the washing up bowl to fit into and a rack on which to place the clean dishes, with my nimble fingers and love of knots mostly producing a sturdy and safe gadget.

It seemed no time at all that is was 'beds down' and time for sleep, having first experienced the hessian washing cubicles, each with a tripod on which to balance the enamel washing bowl and a v-shaped tree branch on which to hang your wash bag and towel. No excuse for not washing at our Guide camps.

Our 'lats', I later learned, were very upmarket compared to many Guide latrines. Yes, we had the obligatory trench but we had individual hessian cubicles, each with a very posh toilet seat, the framework of which stretched across the trench with a toilet seat shaped hole in the strategic place. These proved to be most comfortable and could definitely be classed as 'the thrones' of the 6th Plumstead Common Guides. No soggy loo roll for us either, though in those days, toilet paper was not the soft variety we expect today. It was always kept dry, though, in a lidded tin with string threaded through to hang on the framework.

To complete the cubicle was the small hand spade. This was used to cover what we had 'left behind' in the trench. If a wet camp, this could prove to be quite difficult as, instead of fine, dry soil – easy to sprinkle - there would be heavy clods of damp mud, which made for difficulties in 'covering up' and which inevitably led to sticky, muddy, heavy boots after a 'lat visit'. We were never allowed to forget to wash our hands as, outside the latrines, there was yet another tripod with enamel bowl and a jug of clean water.

So, with our visits to the lats and wash tents over, it was time for bed and what excitement for us first time campers. Such a lot to learn – 'don't touch the sides of the tent' – 'why'- because if you do, the rain will come in, 'make sure your bedding is on your groundsheet' – 'why' – because if you don't, your bedding will get damp; 'put your clothes in your rucksack'– 'why' – because they will get damp too. This was a whole new adventure.

I had already learned how to make up my bed during our weekly Guide meetings. We didn't have sleeping bags, as in later years. Our beds were made from two blankets folded and pinned around a sheet bag, using very large safety pins, kilt pins I called them. Our pillow was tucked into the top. So we rolled out our beds, tried to grab sufficient space in the tent and settled down for the night.

I suppose I must have slept, since morning came around very quickly. It could have been that we didn't go to sleep very early as it was such fun in the dark, flashing our newly acquired torches to make patterns on the tent roof. I remember, when morning came, that it felt damp and my hair was such a tangle. It was the days when I had long hair in ringlets. Mum had always brushed my hair each morning and here I was at camp with Mum far away – so, I tried as best I could. And after all, this was camp and no one minded if you didn't look as smart as you did at weekly meetings.

Breakfast and chores

I soon became used to sitting in the 'horseshoe' for meals and so breakfast came and went in true Guide fashion. We were the orderlies for breakfast, which necessitated looking after our sister Guides and making sure they were served with the food they required.

Once eating had finished, I learned that a daily ritual was about to begin – that of 'spud peeling'. Whilst in the horseshoe, each Guide had to peel the number of potatoes they felt they would require for later in the day. Once each potato had been peeled, it was lobbed into a large dixie that had been placed in the middle of the horseshoe. Of course, we Guides had to see who could make the biggest splash and if Captain or Lefty got wet in the process then this was a definite bonus.

What a mess

I remember no more about that very first camp except that we must have visited the tuck shop on the Saturday. Sweets had only just come off ration and I spent all my pocket money on Mars Bars. I just loved Mars Bars and still do. We used to share one a week at home during ration time, with Mum cutting off a very small sliver each for my brother and I after tea each evening. So, where did I put my Mars Bars for safety? Under my pillow of course!! Sunday morning came to find mashed and mangled Mars Bars under my head, with a wonderful excuse to eat the ensuing mess. I don't remember not being able to eat breakfast or other meals so all must have been well with my digestive system, but my tangled ringlets had small globules of Mars Bar linking the strands of hair – such a sticky, gooey mess! I learned from this experience – to find a safer 'safe' place for my possessions at camp.

Rain, rain and more rain

It rained – but it had to rain at my first camp didn't it. Wellies and waterproofs on and great fun. In later years, at summer camps when it rained, we didn't bother with waterproofs – just putting on our swimming costumes instead. I hasten to add that we did have to wear more suitable attire if 'wooding' or cooking. Captain was always very safety conscious.

How quickly that first camp went and the next one seemed so far away, but it was the first of so many wonderful happy camps. Mum was really interested to hear about it as she had gone camping in those very early days of Guiding.

In her day, instead of travelling in a furniture van, Mum would have loaded up a trek cart and then pushed it all the way to the camping field. Her 'mattress' was a palliasse filled with straw whilst mine was the hard ground or, in later years, a lilo and even later – a camp bed!

I don't remember where my first summer camp was held though it would have been in Kent or Sussex. Over the years, we went to Wivelsfield, Bekesbourne, Plumpton, Waddesdon and, of course, Cudham. Camping was such fun and in later years, as a Guide, I so enjoyed being in charge of my patrol and passing on my acquired camping skills to members of my patrol.

I remember before one camp, Captain sent me to buy some liquid paraffin. I knew Dad used paraffin at home so off I went to the hardware shop. Such embarrassment. Of course, I was redirected to the chemist. I didn't tell Captain!

One camp, at Plumpton, coincided with our family holiday we had each year at Lydd-on-Sea. I was allowed to spend a night at camp in the early part of the week. It had been particularly wet and when my parents arrived to take me back to Lydd they discovered that Captain and Lefty were having great difficulty in keeping us all dry and keeping the fire alight. Of course, no fire – no hot food or water. So, we left the camp with three extra Guides and bedding in order to dry them out and warm them up back at our holiday bungalow. For the rest of the week, Dad and I travelled back and forth from the camp, delivering Guides, bedding and clothes. We had no car so we quickly became acquainted with country bus times and routes. This just couldn't happen nowadays with all the rules and regulations.

Nearly put off for life

Apart from my very first camp at Cudham, I have to admit that I never really enjoyed camping there. I attended several Division, maybe County camps too, at Cudham and one in particular, for Patrol Leaders, was not a particularly happy experience, and nearly put me off camping for life.

Just prior to the camp, I had needed a new 'windcheater', the then current name for 'waterproofs'. I had gone with Mum to buy one and the best bargain was a turquoise colour – kingfisher blue to be precise, and an apt name as, by this time, I was Patrol Leader of the Kingfishers. I just loved the colour but felt sure that I ought to have navy blue, being more of a Guide colour. However, turquoise won the day, even though I did feel slightly awkward that it was not a suitable Guide hue. Captain didn't seem to mind so I became used to wearing this rather bright colour for wet or cold Guide activities. Afterall, it was a shade of blue! But then came the Patrol Leaders' camp at Cudham.

I hadn't felt truly comfortable at this camp and neither had my friend Ann. Our Captain always ran very organised and efficient camps, with each Guide being encouraged to take part and learn all those necessary camping skills in a reassuring and caring environment. The CAs (Camp Advisers), at this particular patrol leaders' camp, seemed very officious and rather frightening. Ann and I had attended many Camps by this time and we felt we had a good knowledge of the way to 'Guide Camp' but, try as we might, we could do nothing right.

During that never ending weekend, I remember being sent to our tent to fetch our waterproofs. I emerged wearing my lovely turquoise windcheater and it was then that I wished the ground would open up and swallow me. What a scene. I was humiliated in front of all the other Guides, and adults too, because my windcheater was not a suitable colour. 'Whatever was my Captain thinking in allowing me to come to camp at Cudham wearing such a colour'. For someone like me, who took such great pride in her appearance as a Guide, this was just complete and utter mortification. Thank goodness, over the ensuing years, the relationship between Guides and their leaders took on a different perspective.

Taken in our front garden in 1957

Sadly, this was the last camp I was to attend as a Guide as, soon after, our beloved Captain moved away from the area and we had no one to take us camping or restore our faith in camping. Of course, I could have attended Division camps or taken my Patrol Leader's Camping Permit so I could take my patrol away, but neither Ann nor I wished to be humiliated further by meeting up with those two fearsome CA sisters who made our camping life so uncomfortable at Cudham. It took much persuasion by my Ranger group to entice me back to camping, but that's another chapter.

More than just a 'Tenderfoot'

It was at my very first camp at Cudham that I began to prepare in earnest for my 'Second Class Test'. I had already passed the knotting as I had used a packer's knot when tying my camp bedding roll at the weekly meeting before going to camp. I had also shown Captain that I could use a reef knot, sheet bend, clove hitch, timber hitch, bowline, fisherman's and round turn and two half hitches.

At camp, each patrol had to take it in turns to 'hoist the colours' every morning before breakfast, so it wasn't long before I became adept at tying the colour and hoisting it up the flagpole ready to 'break (the right way up) later. So, this part of the clause was soon ticked off my test card.

Square lashing was also soon completed as I just loved playing with string. I quickly learnt how to make bedding racks and washing up stands, proving to Captain that my newly found skill of lashing was sufficient to pass this part of the test.

So, that was two clauses completed by the time we arrived home. The first clause was so easy – 'pass the Tenderfoot Test'. In the ensuing months, at our weekly meetings, we spent time each week learning and practicing the necessary skills for passing the remaining clauses.

I really enjoyed learning 'Morse Code' and much time was spent in transmitting and receiving messages – using flags or torches initially. We were later to stage a display at an open evening in the Autumn of 1955, showing our expertise in the use of Morse Code. I had been a Guide for almost two years by that time and was a Patrol Second. Dad decided that he would make a Morse Code flasher and buzzer for my patrol to use. He didn't stop at making just one as the other patrols put in their requests too and Dad was happy to oblige. Our plans for a small Morse Code display escalated into a fully blown competition between patrols to see who could send and receive messages in the fastest time. Dad's buzzers/flashers certainly enhanced our experience and made Morse Code activities more enjoyable. Who knows which patrol won the 'competition' but it didn't matter – we all took part and had such fun.

The Intelligence Clause

During our weekly meetings, we often went to Plumstead Common to practice our stalking and tracking in patrols. Half the patrol laid a trail, usually with the Patrol Leader in charge and then the other half, led by the Patrol Second, would try and follow and retrieve the message that was invariably hidden somewhere near the 'I have gone home' sign. This was great fun and, though we didn't realise at the time, we were developing our leadership and co-operation skills.

I remember making a booklet about '12 living things'. I have to admit, that though I love the countryside and all therein, I still do not remember many names of trees, birds or flowers. So, my booklet was rather an easy way for me to pass this part of the test as I loved finding out information from books and tracing and colouring pictures.

It was, and still is, the remembering of names that I find incredibly difficult, as my long time Guiding friends will tell you. Birds are birds, trees are trees and flowers are flowers, but I cannot remember many of their individual names.

I've already mentioned Morse Code and, despite the time taken in learning it, this was fun, but I wasn't totally sure of its relevance. Not long after I passed this part of the test, the Guide Association decided to remove this clause from the 'Second Class Test'.

Handicraft

The knotting part of the test was easy for me and I enjoyed helping Guides master this skill for many years. I can't count the number of 'knotting boards' I made over the years. At camp, I could often be found 'playing' with string when not sitting whittling a piece of wood.

Fire lighting and cooking was a different matter and I'm not really sure that I did master using just two matches, though I suppose I must have done as Captain was always very strict with us when in testing mode. More about cooking later!

Health

We were certainly fit in those days as we were always playing running about games or going out of the meeting place to practice Scout's Pace. My most favourite game of all was 'hats and no hats' and I continued to enjoy this game for many years to come. It proved invaluable during my teaching career when too wet for netball outside. I always felt very sorry for classes bordering the various school halls as 'hats and no hats' was a very competitive and noisy game. At school I called it 'bands and no bands' (see appendix for rules).

Of course, another favourite game had to be 'ladders' – still popular today. A close third was 'horses and riders' followed by 'cat and mouse' and its alternative version on a circle. Also popular was 'fishes'.

With our meetings it wasn't long before I passed 'Scout's Pace', which left just the 'Rules of Health' to come to terms with before 'Health' could be ticked off.

Service

First Aid seemed to be a winter activity, when it was too cold and dark to go outside. The father of Margaret, one of our Guides, was a St John Ambulance instructor and he would come for weeks at a time to instruct us and supervise our bandaging. I became quite adept at putting on slings and bandaging ankles with triangular bandages. Of course, we were meant to use our Guide ties but no one was going to spoil my 'pristine' and beautifully tied tie. Mum found me a real triangular bandage and this always travelled to Guides with me, to save my precious Guide tie.

Making my 'Morse flag' was not such a challenge for me as I so enjoyed making things. It was good fun, once there were several flags, to use these as well as the buzzers that Dad had made.

Poor Brown Owl – having to answer the telephone at least six times during a space of time on a Monday evening, when we Guides were trying to pass our 'telephoning'. Guides of today will find this clause hard to believe as they seem to have been born with telephones attached to their ears. But for us Guides in the 1950s, the telephone was new contraption as, in its early days, it was only the very rich that could afford such luxury. We Guides had to master buttons A and B in a call box and try not to lose our money before we had relayed the appropriate message.

So, the day came when I passed all the clauses and I became a 'Second Class Guide'. That was such a proud moment when Captain presented me with my oval, navy, cloth badge with its green trefoil in the centre. I had to ensure that it was sewn on to the left sleeve, below the shoulder knot. The next part of my Guiding journey could begin.

More than just a Second Class Guide

Now that I had achieved my Second Class, I could search through the badge book and choose which proficiency badges interested me.

I began with concentrating on 'The Little House Emblem' which was gained by passing Child Nurse, Cook, Homemaker, Hostess, Laundress and Needlewoman, though my very first proficiency badge was Knitter. My friends, as they read this, won't be a bit surprised to hear that.

I'm a failure – well, it felt like it!

I was to experience my first 'failure' as a Guide on the initial occasion I went to take my Cooks Badge. We had to go to the local rectory, where the vicar's wife was to test us. There were four of us who went along one Monday instead of attending the Guide meeting. Though Mum had allowed me to practice making cakes at home, I was not very confident but Mum assured me that all would be well. 'After all', she said, 'you won't be expected to cook anything without a recipe'. How wrong she was.

My first task was to make a sponge cake. I suppose I should have known the proportions of butter to sugar, eggs and flour but sadly I did not. So that disaster was followed by the request to make custard, Now I knew how to make custard but I was, by then, in such a tizzy that I completely forgot to add the sugar, and this was sufficient to cause me to fail. Oh dear. That failure was to have a profound effect on my 'cooking confidence' – even to this day. Thank goodness that achieving badges is now so different.

After that, I concentrated on the five Little House Badges until the day came when I needed to try again with my 'Cooks', the one remaining, and the one stopping me from being presented with that lovely Little House Emblem.

I had hoped for a different tester but no such luck! The appointed day came when I had to present myself to the rectory for my retest. I had practiced, learned recipes off by heart – including oven temperatures – and worked myself up into a frenzy. I needed to pass this badge. There is definitely truth in the old adage, 'practice makes perfect', together with the saying, 'it at first you don't succeed, try, try, again. I was successful on my second attempt and from this experience I learnt to face challenges positively and not to give up on things.

I looked at the Woodcraft Emblem next but my inability to remember names of natural things made this an impossibility. That was just too much of a challenge for me.

I gained my Thrift badge and, prior to the test, I recall going out with Ann during the school holidays. We traipsed around the streets with an old pram, knocking on doors to collect jars and newspapers. We were 'salvaging' – one of the clauses we needed to pass.

My article, made from things that would otherwise be thrown away, was a patchwork blanket made from squares of my outgrown dresses and school blouses. An old curtain formed the backing. This became my camp blanket and it was on to the curtain side that I began to sew my ever increasing number of badges, collected specifically for this purchase. Pride of place went to Mum's Ranger and Guider badges, followed closely by my Brownie badges. So, we were 'going green' and 'recycling' even in those far off days.

This blanket was to last many years before my collection of badges grew too numerous and more space was needed.

It was as a Guider that I purchased an army surplus blanket and transferred my ever increasing collection. Sadly, when we last moved house, I discovered that my precious blanket had been attacked by moths. Not wanting to transfer the dreaded moths to our new property, I decided to keep those wonderful memories, contained on my blanket, in my head, and so my collection went to the 'happy home' for moth eaten blankets and badges'.

I am so sad about this – so many memories confined to the dustbin – but the moths just had to go'.

Busy, busy, busy

Soon after, I began to work on the achievement of my 'First Class' Badge. Three clauses were already complete – including that dreaded Cook's Badge, thank goodness.

My next major challenge was learning to swim. My friend Ann could already swim the required 50 yards as her Mum was a proficient swimmer, so it was Ann's Mum who came to the rescue. She agreed to take those Guides wishing to learn to the Public Baths in Woolwich on a Sunday morning. What a good teacher she was, one who was sympathetic to our fears and needs. It took us quite a time to achieve our goal of the required 50 yard swim but most of us acquired the necessary skill. It was certainly worth getting up at 6.00am on a Sunday morning so that lessons were over and we were home in time for breakfast before heading off to our church services.

I bought my own copies of 'Scouting for Boys' and 'The Wolf that Never Sleeps' so I could read and discover more about our founder BP. I was well on the way to gaining the required knowledge for the First Class Badge when Captain announced that she was retiring from work and leaving the area. We were devastated. Our role model and 'Guiding rock' was leaving us. Not only was Captain leaving but Lefty had decided to leave too. Who was to take on these roles? No one came forward. We were bereft.

It seemed like the end of the world but then we were thrown a life line. Brown Owl, whose daughter was, by this time, a Guide, said that she would become the leader but would need all the help she could get from Patrol Leaders. She already had Brownies to organize and couldn't possibly organise a weekly Guide meeting at the same time.

So, leadership skills to the fore. I found myself helping to run the Guides alongside my fellow Patrol Leaders. Ann and I organised and planned our weekly meetings with Brown Owl there as the 'adult in charge'. We enjoyed this experience and it certainly made me realise that this was what I wanted to do in the future – become a Guide Leader.

The First Class Test preparation was shelved and I never did achieve this as a Guide, though I later gained the badge as a Ranger.

Looking wider

Our weekly meetings were such fun but there were also opportunities to meet with other Guides beyond the confines of our meeting place. I've already mentioned the Patrol Leaders' Camp at Cudham – but that is one I wish to forget.

We had District gatherings, for events such as Thinking Day. All I remember about these is the singing. It was at such gatherings that I learnt 'proper Guide songs'. We didn't seem to spend much time, on those occasions, singing the raucous Scout songs. I enjoyed compiling my own song book and to sharing these songs with our own Guides.

Thinking Day was always a special day, though I can't remember ever celebrating in our own Guide Company. I always enjoyed wearing my Guide uniform to school and being allowed out of school to attend the Westminster Abbey 'laying of the wreaths' ceremony held, in those days, on Thinking Day at 11.00am. This was just a very short and simple ceremony and any member in uniform could go. There were never many there but I really enjoyed feeling part of something much bigger than just my own Guide Company.

I suppose I was incredibly fortunate to be just a short bus ride away from school to Westminster Abbey and in having a sympathetic Headmistress who allowed us to miss lessons, in order to attend this short service each year, until I left school. After that, and once it became 'ticket only', I tried every year to obtain the necessary ticket, though not always successfully.

Before our Captain left, we took part in a rally at Catford Stadium, in 1957, to commemorate the Centenary of BP. We had to dress as Scouts and were in the pageant depicting the very first Scout Rally at Crystal Palace. I remember having to wear my brother's Scout shorts, shirt, neckerchief and hat, and carry a broom handle with notches in it to make it look like a Scout staff. Each of us Guides had one and I seem to recall that it was rather difficult climbing to the upper deck of the bus on the journey to and from Catford, whilst holding 'our staffs' and trying not to cause injury to other passengers.

On another occasion, Ann and I represented our Division at a service on the other side of London. I can't recall why this was being held but I can remember sitting up in the church balcony and watching all the standards being processed to the altar. What a spectacular sight. Maybe this was 1957 too.

It was about this time that I began to go with Ann to the 'Saturday Night Dances', organized by the Scouts, and held at King's Warren School on the other side of Plumstead Common. Of course, all the Guides sat on one side of the hall and the Scouts on the other but those brave enough did mix with the opposite sex and good, innocent fun was had by all.

My life long friend, Yvonne, and I still reminisce about these dances and talk about how my mother wouldn't allow me to wear stockings. I would set off from home wearing ankle socks and remove them once out of sight! Oops, that was the 1st Guide Law not adhered to.

Life after Captain

Brown Owl eventually 'handed over' to an ex Guide who came to 'take us on'. This was short lived as she soon gave birth to her first child and left us. Then came along Jean - of 'Golden Earrings' fame from the Gang Show during my first weeks as a Guide. Jean had since married and had two young boys. Her husband was willing to baby sit each Monday, so we had a Captain again. I still remember planning Guide activities for the weekly meetings but, as Jean was a new leader, perhaps she was glad of the help.

Guide life jogged along quite happily after that and all too soon, it seemed, it was time for me to leave as I had reached that age when I was too old. I was approaching my 16th birthday.

I had heard that there were Sea Rangers who met in the Academy buildings on Woolwich Common. And so began the next phase of my Guiding Journey.

**'For we are all sisters in this World Guiding Movement,
Learning and Loving in all that we do'**

Chapter Three

'Today I'm a Ranger living for Service'

I knew that Ann wasn't too keen on becoming a Ranger but she promised to come with me for a time. So, in January, 1959, we set off for the next part of our Guiding journey. It was rather daunting, as we had very little idea of exactly where the Rangers met and we certainly knew none of the members. I was so pleased that Ann had kept her word and had come with me.

We eventually found where they were. The Academy Buildings were a maze of rooms occupied by the Army. Fortunately, the security man on the gate pointed us in the right direction and we eventually found the meeting room and opened the door timidly to see if we had indeed come to the right place. We had – such a relief.

We found our way in through this door and seemed to disappear into a maze of corridors

The Rangers looked so mature and smart. Whilst Guides, we were used to seeing mostly Guide blue blouses and brightly coloured ties. Here, we were greeted by 'adults' all dressed in sombre navy blue jumpers and skirts, with black neckerchiefs rolled like the Scouts and white fancy lanyards criss-crossing them. On their heads they wore 'sailor hats'. I had seen pictures of Sea Rangers, including photographs of the Queen and Princess Margaret, but I had never met any until that day in January.

HRS Princess Elizabeth
(now HM The Queen)
as a
Sea Ranger

This was so different to any Guide meetings we had been to and, because Ann and I had taken a major part in running our meetings, we felt quite awkward and unsure of ourselves, no longer being in control. We were spectators for that first evening, simply soaking up the situation and trying to come to terms with the fact that we didn't know anyone or really understand what was happening.

That was the last meeting Ann was to come to as she decided that 'Sea Rangering' wasn't for her. I decided to persevere – something that Guiding had already instilled in me. It wasn't long before I had made friends and was beginning to understand the different terminology and proceedings. I have so much to thank Guiding for. My confidence and self-esteem had grown enormously since those early Brownie days and my previous Guiding experiences had equipped me to take on unknown challenges fairly confidently. So, before long, I was invested as a Sea Ranger and became a member of Starboard Watch and the crew of SRS Superb.

Sea Sense

I was soon to learn that the Sea Ranger's 'bible' was entitled 'Sea Sense' and I eventually bought my own copy. It was rather dismaying to read that,

> *'It is essential that those thinking of becoming Sea Rangers should have a sea sense, a love of ships and all to do with them. They must be prepared to read and study; to meet and mix with those who sail in big and little ships; and to find in them the common bond which unites all sea-loving people'.*

The nearest I had been to the sea was family holidays at Lydd-on-Sea, Kent, but my enjoyment came from looking at it and definitely not being in it. I had enjoyed the Cross Channel ferries to Dover and the Isle of Wight ferry so I was not deterred from becoming a member, though my interest lay more in the Girl Guide aspect than the sea. There were no Land Ranger or Cadet companies near, so Sea Rangers it had to be.

I confess that during the years of being a Sea Ranger I didn't once set foot in a boat, though I learnt all the technical terms – the rules of the sea, how to use a boatswain's call and its various 'pipes', the international Code of Signals, watch times, definitions of different boats and associated terminology and much, much more. My knotting skills were enhanced and I loved making my lanyards with intricate knots and use of the 'Turk's Head'. Morse and semaphore were quickly revised and I learned enough to pass my OSR (Ordinary Sea Ranger) badge.

I enjoyed the discipline associated with Sea Rangering – the salute akin to the Naval Salute and saluting the quarterdeck, 'manning the ship' and the ship's bell, being organized into watches, having a Skipper and Number One, following 'ship's time' and marching with thumbs tucked in and arms raised to nose level.

There was a special event held in Greenwich at the Royal Naval College. I cannot recall what it was but I do remember spending several evenings at the Naval College, learning how to march in true naval fashion. The occasion came, we marched impeccably and then took part in a service in the beautiful and impressive Royal Naval Chapel. How sad that I do not remember what this was all about.

I might be a Sea Ranger but I'm still a Girl Guide

I was able, as a Ranger, to continue working on the Guide Training Programme and I soon discovered that I could resume working for my First Class badge. This had been curtailed when a Guide because Captain and Lefty had left us and, as a Patrol Leader, I had taken on the responsibility of having a major part in running the company, which left no time for passing tests.

I remember spending hours compiling a 'History of Guiding', one of the required clauses, and including comprehensive written details, supplemented with pictures, photographs and drawings. My Division Commissioner asked to borrow this for a display at one Division AGM at Woolwich Town Hall. Whilst we Rangers were hostessing, my precious book disappeared – never to be found again. The Commissioner was mortified and so was I. However, a Guide sings and smiles under all difficulties and I tried hard to 'forgive and forget'.

Badge testing day arrived and entailed a trip to Eltham. Fortunately, I still had my 'History of Guiding' at that time to prove that I had collected the necessary information. Many Guides and Rangers were there and we were dispersed into various rooms of the hall, where testers were waiting to interrogate us or give us practical tasks to do.

All that was left to do, by the end of the day, was to undertake the 'First Class Hike'. This was completed several weeks later, necessitating a trip to Chislehurst to await instructions as to the route to follow. Jean and Celia, my fellow Rangers, made up my team, and I passed – even the cooking clause!!

I felt enormously proud being presented with my badge during a Division event, and of having my photograph taken by a reporter from our local paper- the 'Kentish Independent'. It was wonderful to be able to sew the badge on to the back of my neckechief and, at that time, I was the only Ranger in my crew to have achieved this.

Leading on from the Guide First Class, I continued to challenge myself by working towards the necessary requirements for the Ranger Service Star.

I began with something I was confident about – craft and needlework. This involved making an outfit to wear, using a sewing machine as well as hand sewing, to show a range of stitches and techniques. I remember the skirt and top – made from material obtained from 'Stan's Stall' in Woolwich Covered Market. It was green, merging with peachy-pink colours and had a full skirt loosely pleated into a waist band.

The top needed to show buttonholes and have inset sleeves. As soon as the garment had been passed by the tester, I removed the sleeves as I really wanted a sleeveless top. To complete the outfit, I knitted a peach-coloured jacket and so this, together with various other requirements, enabled me to pass my Dressmaker's Certificate.

One clause of three was now completed for part one of the service star. On to the second clause – and for this I worked on the Community Service Certificate. Just one more to go – but what was it to be?

Return to Camping

Jean, the Boatswain of our Starboard watch, began to plan a camp at Cudham so that she could be assessed for her Ranger Campcraft Certificate and Permit. She hoped that all members of the watch would give their support and was very surprised and dismayed when I initially refused to go. I explained my reasons, having been totally 'put off' camping, especially at Cudham, by those two CA ogres when a Guide.

Fortunately, Jean had very persuasive powers and assured me that her camp would be nothing like that fateful one. I went and thank goodness I did as my faith in Guide camping was restored. I later achieved my Campcraft Certificate in Herefordshire whilst being an adopted 'Land Ranger' when at college, and this completed the last requirement for the Ranger Service Star part one.

Once Jean passed her test, we went for several lightweight weekend camps and also Rover/Ranger Camps at Downe, the Scout Campsite near Cudham. What fun we had.

I even acted as assistant quartermaster for Plumstead Common District Camp one summer holiday. So, not only was I camping away from Rangers who had renewed my confidence in camping, but I was helping to cook too. This was certainly a personal challenge for me but one I relished, and I thoroughly enjoyed the experience. I am so grateful to Jean for enticing me back to camping.

QM and AQM (unbelievably I was AQM).
I loved my summer uniform – a white shirt

More to Rangers than just meetings in Woolwich

1960 saw many celebrations for the 50th Anniversary of the Guide Association – the Golden Jubilee. Empire Pool, Wembley, was the venue for 'The Birthday Festival', which included the 'Carnival of Badges' and 'The Journey of Soy'. This took place on 21st, 22nd, 23rd July.

Rangers were needed to be stewards and sell programmes and, much to the amazement of my school friends, I declined the invitation to attend the annual sixth form dance at St. Olave's and St. Saviour's Grammar School for Boys in Tooley Street, London Bridge. This was the 'other half' of my secondary school, St. Saviour's and St. Olave's Grammar School for Girls, situated at the junction of the New Kent Road, Old Kent Road and Tower Bridge Road. Having promised to help, I could not go back on my word so 'The Journey of Soy' took precedence over the school dance and, after all, I felt as I was taking part in a small piece of Guiding history.

The whole experience was fantastic – just feeling part of the Golden Jubilee Celebrations, watching the pageant for its many performances and meeting so many interesting people. I just loved it.

Another fantastic experience was selling programmes to the crowds in Parliament Square for the Wedding of Princess Margaret to Anthony Armstrong-Jones on May 6th 1960. We met at Guide Headquarters at the crack of dawn, where we were given our instructions for the day. We then proceeded to Parliament Square and soon built up a rapport with the policemen and soldiers lining the square.

APPROVED SOUVENIR PROGRAMME
PUBLISHED BY GRACIOUS PERMISSION OF
HER MAJESTY QUEEN ELIZABETH THE QUEEN MOTHER

THE WEDDING OF HER ROYAL HIGHNESS

THE PRINCESS MARGARET

AND MR

ANTONY ARMSTRONG-JONES

IN WESTMINSTER ABBEY
6 MAY 1960

KING GEORGE'S JUBILEE TRUST
THREE SHILLINGS AND SIXPENCE

We were allowed on the inside of the barrier and had such fun talking and bantering with the crowds, many of whom had camped out all night. The weather was warm and I felt so smart in my Sea Ranger Summer Uniform – white shirt for summer instead of the navy jumper. Lunch was a picnic on the library floor back at CHQ. Another amazing experience.

Cream cakes and a collection

During the Golden Jubilee year, a Division Service was held in St. Mary's Church, Woolwich, conducted by the controversial Revd. Nick Stacey, who later left the ministry and became Deputy Director of OXFAM.

One of our duties, as Rangers, was to undertake the collection during the final hymn. I remember sitting on the right hand side of the church, in about the third row from the front so that I would be ready to 'cover' the first six rows, before processing with the collection bag to the altar.

The service began, the colours were received, hymns and prayers followed and then the sermon. It was then that I began to feel rather unwell. I swallowed hard in the hope that my nausea would pass – but sadly it didn't. Very quickly I realised I needed to make an immediate, and very hasty exit, from the church. Fortunately, there was a side door almost adjacent to my pew. I hoped (and prayed) that it would open easily and I just made it outside before my stomach emptied its contents into the flower bed by the door. Once that was over, I felt so much better and hoped to creep back in unnoticed, but a very kindly verger had come out to make sure all was well. He was so concerned and I was so embarrassed.

I returned to my pew, comfortable once more, and was just in time to carry out my 'collecting' duties – fortunately. The moral of this story – never eat out of date cream cakes in the sixth form common room at school!!

It's a 'lock out' !

There was to be a weekend at Foxlease soon after the embarrassing cream-cake episode in St. Mary's Church, and several of our crew attended. It was to be my first visit and I was very excited about seeing Foxlease for the first time. Some of us travelled with Boatswain Jean in her car.

Our lovely 'Foxlease' at Lyndhurst in the picturesque New Forest

I cannot remember anything about the training but I do know that we slept in the attic where, eventually, the younger members of staff slept before they moved into the Lodge. It was definitely 'all in together girls' – one open space under the beams of the roof with us Rangers fitting in as best as we could.

On the Saturday evening, Jean organized a 'night out' for those interested in accompanying her after the final session of the day and our evening meal. We were going to the local 'pub' to liven up the weekend. This was a new experience; my parents wouldn't have approved and my Boatswain was trying to lead me astray! Until then, my behavior at any Guide function had always been impeccable. Oh dear.

Our 'night out venue'

We walked up the road to 'The Crown Stirrup' and enjoyed one or two drinks, not that I remember what we had. Last call came for orders so time to be heading back. We crept and giggled our way 'home' – and then discovered we were locked out! Whoops. What were we to do? Lots of 'sshhhhs' and giggles, as you may imagine, and then we found the back outside stairs.

We were trying to be so very quiet. We made our way up the stairs and hoped the door at the top would be open. It wasn't – but – it did open and there to greet us was the Guider in Charge !! To say that 'she was not amused' is an understatement. We were dispatched to our beds, having been told that, 'we should be thoroughly ashamed of ourselves'.

We tried to creep up the stairs and we tried not to giggle too much either, but that's not easy is it? Our beds found, we soon fell into them and slept soundly. Sadly, a little too soundly as we overslept on the Sunday morning and missed colours. That would have been 'sin enough' but WE WERE THE COLOUR PARTY'!!

It was to be 24 years before I returned to Foxlease. Shame and the Guider in Charge sadly being the deterrent. But what lessons I was learning through my Guiding – lessons that were to have a profound effect on the way I dealt with problems and difficulties in the future. I always try to empathise with those I come into contact with , endeavouring to find out, and understand, the reasons for various behaviours.

On to pastures new

Soon after the Foxlease episode, I left school and prepared for my next journey through life – that of going to Teacher Training College. I didn't have to leave Rangers and promised faithfully to visit during college holidays. And so it was, in September 1961, that I set off from Paddington Station to catch the steam train to Hereford to begin my next adventure.

I had already spoken about Guiding to one of the college lecturers who had interviewed me prior to my acceptance. I am convinced that Guiding secured my place at Hereford. Miss Bewsher, art lecturer, was the local Commissioner and quickly found me a Guide Unit in the City. This was the start of a very long friendship with Smos, the Captain of 10th Hereford, St. Nicholas Guide Company. We kept in touch until she passed away in 2015. Smos also ran the Hereford City Division Land Ranger Company and I became an 'adopted member' – a 'Sland Ranger'. It was wonderful to be able to join in Ranger activities whilst at college, as well as at home in the holidays.

I had come such a long way since first becoming a member of the Guide Association, way back in 1949. Even during my Ranger days, I owed so much to my Guiding – through the opportunities to give service and develop leadership and social skills. Guiding, for me, was going from strength to strength.

**'Rangering forth
I will go where life leads'**

Chapter Four

'Today an Assistant, learning whilst leading'

That Great Sisterhood of Guiding

And so I embarked on the next stage of my life – and Guiding too. I was away from home for the first time, learning to live in an all-female community of diverse personalities, with many and varied accents. This was Hereford Training College, situated on a hill above the beautiful City of Hereford, with its friendly people readily welcoming me. I was surrounded by unbelievably picturesque countryside – such a oontrast to South East London. I just loved it.

Smos quickly took me under her wing and collected me each week in her Mini to take me to the Guide meetings. Though Smos lived fairly close to college, Guides met on the other side of Hereford City, just by the old bridge crossing the River Wye, so a ride in Smos' car was much appreciated.

The first thing I noticed about the Guides was their red and white striped ties. I had only seen the normal colours of Guide ties up until then, mainly green, yellow or red. These striped ties were most impressive. I quickly learned that special permission had been granted for these unorthodox ties as the Company was attached to St. Nicholas Church and the colours represented Saint Nicholas and his association with Father Christmas.

It didn't take me long to 'find my feet' and I was soon taking a major part in the running of the Guide meetings, under the supervision of Smos, of course. What a superb role model she was. Over the years, I learned so much from her and am so grateful to her for readily accepting this stranger from London.

It was whilst with St' Nicholas Guides that I became known as 'Bov'. The Guides called Smos 'Smos', not Captain, and they didn't want to call me Avril, so – Avril – Bovril – Bov. I'm still called this today by a few.

Smos soon persuaded me to work towards the achievement of my warrant as Lieutenant and the Christmas vacation saw me heading back to London, Victoria, to buy my Guider's blouse, tie and hat in the CHQ shop.

17 – 19 Buckingham Palace Road.

Commonwealth HQ, which used to be called Imperial HQ

This tradition of visiting the Guide Shop at Victoria continued for many years as my daughter, Karyn, whose uniforms were also bought on visits to London, journeyed there with her daughters, Abiee and Louisa, to do the same.

My Warrant Badge – worn under the knot of my Guider's tie

The joys of singing

In that Spring term of 1962, there was a Division Camp Fire Singing Competition, which I later discovered had been initiated by Smos to encourage more singing in the units. What fun we had in learning new songs and deciding what to sing for the competition. This was 'right up my street'.

We had to perform national and international songs as part songs and rounds in the District Heats before being selected to represent the Division in the County Final. I'm not sure of the outcome, though I know we passed our County Camp Fire Singing Certificate during the course of the competition.

Our repertoire included – as far as I can remember:

Swinging Along (part song)
Glory to Thee my God this night (round)
Waltzing Matilda (song from another Country)
I like the flowers (part song)
Heidi (part song)
Norwegian Echo (free choice)
Belgian Conga (action song)

These are still some of my favourites today, with the exception of Waltzing Matilda, which I find really tedious to sing.

It was wonderful to be part of a 'Singing Company' but even more so was that Smos was the 'Campfire Leader' for the County and travelled throughout Herefordshire and the neighbouring counties of Worcestershire and Gloucestershire, leading camp-fires great and small. She always asked me to accompany her, and I loved every minute of the singing and of meeting so many fellow Guides, Rangers and Guiders in the process, not to mention tearing through the country lanes in her mini, trying to find the various meeting places and camp sites.

And so began my interest in the leading of camp-fire singing.

The Royal Albert Hall

As well as having a 'Singing Guide Company', Smos also ran a 'Singing Ranger Company', and this resulted in the Rangers' visit to London to take part in 'Encore', the combined Rover/Ranger Music Festival held at the Royal Albert Hall. As I was only an 'adopted' Hereford City Land Ranger, I couldn't join them on stage but I was able to support them and watch the festival from the Royal Box.

Yes, Herefordshire had been allocated the Royal Box for the duration of the festival. Obviously, we didn't share it with Her Majesty, but we felt 'very Royal'. Guiding, indeed, provides many opportunities that wouldn't otherwise happen.

The Rangers were staying at BP House, not too far from the Royal Albert Hall, so it was good to meet them there before and after the performance, though it meant a late night for me as the journey back to Woolwich necessitated two buses to Charing Cross, a train to Woolwich Arsenal Station and another bus up the hill. But, it was so worth it.

A 'Sland Ranger'

Whenever College commitments allowed, I 'gatecrashed' the Land Ranger meetings and was made to feel so much part of their company. They christened me a 'Sland Rnger' – S(ea) Land – and for three years, whilst at college, I took part in their activities as much as I could. Land Rangering, for me, felt much more comfortable than Sea Rangering, though I hasten to add, I was enormously grateful that there were Rangers in Woolwich, albeit Sea Rangers.

Hereford City Division was to hold a camp at Lugwardine, not far out of the city, and the Rangers were going. Several of them were to be assessed for their Ranger Campcraft Certificate, as Jean had a few years before. I joined in with the camp, just to go and enjoy myself, but I was soon persuaded, when there, to take my test too. Unlike my Land Ranger friends, I had not prepared for this but felt I had nothing to lose by trying.

It was rather daunting, thinking on my feet when being assessed for knowledge of food values, good fire-lighting wood, tent pitching, tent repairs, gadget making and programme planning. My inability to recognize specific trees proved rather a challenge but, unbelievably, I passed and could hardly wait to return home to tell my Sea Ranger friends of my achievement. I really did have much to thank Boatswain Jean for.

Lost a night!

We weren't really but could easily have been.

There was an incident night hike in collaboration the City Rover Scouts. Wow – this could not pass without joining in now could it?

It was difficult to persuade the college authorities that no harm was going to befall me. Thy were so protective in the early 1960s, I suppose still being in *'loco parentis'* until we reached the age of 21, so extra nights away from college were rather difficult.

Permission was eventually given and I joined up the City Land Rangers to travel to our meeting place for 11.00pm. We were divided into teams of four – two Rangers and two Rovers, given our preliminary instructions and then we waited, for what we were not sure.

Eventually, our team was called. We were led outside and blindfolded, then bundled into a car and set off in the hands of our driver, one of the Rover Scouters. After much jolting and juddering and the inevitable hilarity, we were told to leave the car and given maps. What a blessing we had our torches with us. So, the object of the exercise was to find our way back to our original meeting place, the quickest team arriving back being the victors.

 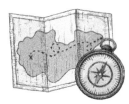

Well, I hadn't a clue where we were! Afterall, I was a 'townie'. I didn't know the wilds of Herefordshire and it was so dark. I obviously didn't eat my carrots when younger as I couldn't, and still can't, see in the dark.

What fun we had, though, and thank goodness for the Rovers who seemed to steer us back eventually, where hot soup and rolls were waiting for us. I arrived back at college just in time for Sunday breakfast.

Another Training Centre

A County Weekend was planned at Broneirion, the Welsh Training Centre at Llandinam.

When asked if I would like to go, I thought of my past experience at a Girl Guide Training Centre - Foxlease, when I went home in 'disgrace' for being locked out. However, I was persuaded and enjoyed a good weekend in a really beautiful house in fantastic surroundings.

I remember spending much time outside in the grounds and of eating a cream-tea on the front lawn, though not about the training we received, but my most vivid memory was again exploding into a fierce fit of giggles. Once I started, I found it so hard to suppress my sniggering shakes. Thank goodness I have learned more control since, though it does occasionally happen that my giggles can't be supressed and I end up with tears streaming down my face.

However, back to the story.

I was sharing a room with Smos, Pug (Ann) and another Anne, who later became County Commissioner for Herefordshire. We had a delightful room just at the top of the main stairs. In the corner of the room was another door. Of course, inquisitiveness took over and, whilst we were getting ready for bed on our first night, we decided to open it and see what was behind it. Well, there was a 'behind' behind the door – that of one of the Commissioners.

In those days, Commissioners still seemed rather fearsome. Miss P-H was getting ready for bed in her single room and was standing there in her long drawers and, like the Guider in Charge at Foxlease, was 'not amused' when confronted by four pairs of bright and amused eyes peering at her from around the door. We hastily shut the door and collapsed on our beds, the tears streaming down our faces.

Guide Club

Whenever Rangers or Cadets were leaving home to go to college, they were encouraged to join the College Guide Club. That was all well and good if there was one to join. Hereford College didn't have one.

After my first year there, and once I had found my feet, I decided to start one. There were now three years of students at the college. Our senior cohort was the first of the 'three year students' and so student numbers grew by more than a third in my second year. I felt confident that sufficient interest would be shown and so began Hereford Training College Guide Club. I was elected 'President' and had a secretary to assist me.

We met monthly, more for a social chat than anything Guide related but I liaised with Miss Bewsher, our art lecturer and local Commissioner, in order to place students wishing to help with local Brownie Packs or Guide Companies. Some of the students even became Land Rangers with Smos.

At the end of its first year, just before our Summer vacation, we organised a weekend camp at Dinedor Hill, which was great fun. We divided ourselves into patrols, had allocated chores after which we concentrated on woodcraft related activities. Many of us had some sort of 'whittled' souvenir to take back to adorn our rooms. I remember enjoying making the flagpole and then having a colour party to raise and lower the flag at the appropriate time. Peeling potatoes, too, seem to conjure up a vivid memory.

Following on from this successful weekend, we were often to be found at weekends hiking in the locality and staying in Youth Hostels.

Just before I left college to return to Woolwich to teach, the County Commissioner visited us. We entertained her in the Hereford Room and I was amazed at how very red her long nails were. No County Commissioner I have met since has ever had such long painted nails!

Time to say goodbye

It seemed no time at all that my three years at college were over. The time had just flown by. Smos had been a wonderful friend, supporting and encouraging me, not only with Guide related activities but with school affairs too. When my Teaching Practice Schools were in the city, we would meet in Ascaris or the Continental Café, at the end of the school day, for a coffee and a chat.

 Smos taught in a city secondary school and understood, only too well, the trials and tribulations about being on teaching practice. I felt sad that this time was coming to an end but excited at the thought of 'moving on' to another phase of my life and actually having my own class to teach.

My last day at college was a Sunday and our 'Going Down' Service was to be held in the afternoon in Hereford Cathedral. It happened that this Sunday was a Church Parade Sunday too, so the morning saw me dressed in my Guider's uniform at St. Nicholas Church, for my last Church Parade with the Guides. They seemed sorry to see me go and I knew I would miss them. We had enjoyed so much fun together and I promised to return to Hereford on future occasions to visit.

One of my most treasured possessions today is a pair of bookends carved in the shape of trefoils. This was presented to me by my Hereford Guiding friends along with a framed photograph of the Guide Company, including me, as we posed for the Hereford Times newspaper, following the dedication of our company standard. I knew of no other Guide Company with their own Company Standard and we were able to acquire ours by a legacy left to the company by a previous captain, specifically for that purpose.

Smos is standing to the right of the vicar (just reaching his shoulder) and I'm standing to the left of Land Ranger, Helen on the 2nd row.

So, with the Trefoil Bookends and Company Photograph safely packed away, I attended the 'Going Down' Service in the Cathedral on 4th July 1964, and my college days had come to an end.

'All the time knowing that the great game of Guiding
is encouraging Guiders and girls – everywhere'

Chapter Five

'Today I'm a Guider, teaching and leading'

The same but different

September 1964 saw me back in Plumstead embarking upon my chosen career of teaching. My first post was at East Wickham Infant School in Welling, just over the border in Kent, now the London Borough of Bexley, so not far to travel to and from home each day.

Being a newly qualified teacher, I decided that time would no longer allow me to attend Rangers as well as being involved with a Guide Company, so I handed in my Sea Ranger's hat and bade farewell to my fellow Rangers. I enjoyed a really good 'send off', a visit to Streatham Ice Rink with very bruised knees to prove it, and a wonderful visit to London to watch Julie Andrews in 'The Sound of Music'. This has to be one of my all time favourite musicals and I still have vivid memories of us Rangers galloping up the stairs to our upper circle seats.

I had now reached the grand age of 21 and so was deemed old enough to become a Guide Leader. As there were no Guide Companies needing a Captain at that time, I decided to return to my old Guide Company at Wesley Hall, the 6th Plumstead Common Guides, and become their Lieutenant. Jean, of 'Golden Earrings' fame from my first Gang Show, was still Captain and welcomed me back with open arms, having run the company unaided since Ann and I had left five years previously. It was good to be back and that Autumn passed quickly and seemed fairly uneventful.

Jean and I are on the 2nd row

Just before Christmas, the District Commissioner, Miss Holland, visited and explained that a neighbouring Guide Company was to be without a Captain after Christmas and asked if I would be interested in taking it over. I didn't need to be asked twice, and so it was that, in January 1965, I became Captain of the 7th Plumstead Common (St. Margaret's) Guide Company which met on the other side of Plumstead Common and nearer to home. Janet was my Lieutenant.

We did all the usual Guide activities and I remember vividly spending meetings outside on the common or in the woods, learning those necessary woodcraft skills. Fund-raising, too, was a priority and we held many blue and yellow functions (yellow being the company tie colour). The Guides also enjoyed the fairly frequent fund-raising discos which we held nearby in St. James' Church Hall, complete with live band and a 'bouncer', who happened to be Ken, an ex Scouter and still a life long friend.

I continued with St. Margaret's Guides until December, 1966, when my first marriage took place and necessitated a move from London to Staffordshire. My last meeting saw Miss Holland, now the retired District Commissioner, coming to test us for our Company Campfire Singing Certificate. Yes, I had continued with the singing and we were definitely deemed to be a 'singing company'. Smos had taught me well and we passed.

Staffordshire

My Guider's hat was now to be adorned with its third County Badge. First had been the Herefordshire Lion, followed by the London Crest depicting the Tower of London and the River Thames, and now was the Staffordshire knot. It wasn't long before I discovered that there were no Guides in Great Haywood, the village where we lived, not far from Stafford. 'No Guides' I exclaimed. 'Well. That needs to be remedied'. And it was.

Very soon, the 1st Great Haywood Guides held its inaugural meeting with me as Captain and a neighbour as Lieutenant. We were incredibly lucky as, though our meeting hall was very tiny, we had acres of Shugborough Park to explore right on our doorstep. The Earl of Litchfield was very accommodating and allowed us to wander at will through his country estate, ideal for putting into practice, and accomplishing, those necessary Guiding skills.

That first year seemed rather a trial, as far as the Guiding Programme was concerned, because we were eagerly awaiting the launch of the new Guide Handbooks. None of the old syllabi were available and it was to be nearly a year before we received details of the new programme. For a new company, whose members had never been involved with Guiding before, this had been incredibly difficult as no literature was available.

I managed to acquire a few test cards from Jean in London so my Guides could see and feel that they were progressing with their challenges but there was little else. 'Wait until the new handbooks are available' was all we heard. Thank goodness I was confident in assuming that out door activities would still be at the forefront of any new programme. We were able to concentrate on these and be ready for whatever the new programme had in store for us.

Not only was the programme changing, but the uniform too. However, we managed to acquire some old uniforms to keep us going until the new ones became available. It was the first time that I was to experience this secrecy surrounding Girl Guide launches – not a hint of any detail was given. But we survived and I'm sure the Guides didn't realise the difficulties we were having.

1968 eventually arrived, bringing to an end the long wait and the eagerly anticipated launch of the new handbooks, programme and uniform. Hooray.

Reunited

A new marriage, new job, new location and a new house left little time for me to acquire the necessary qualifications to take my Guides camping but a solution was at hand. Smos invited us to join her camp in the Wye Valley. What an adventure for my Guides as few had been away from Staffordshire before.

Wendy, my secondary school friend, had been a Guide and volunteered to accompany us, so one August day we left Great Haywood behind and the Guides embarked on another adventure. We were able to Youth Hostel on the way and spent a few days in North Wales, exploring Snowdonia before joining Smos and her Guides.

Great Haywood Guides were used to singing – are you surprised? So, every evening could be heard the sounds of campfire sings echoing around wherever we happened to be. Of course, once we had met up with Smos, the volume increased, as did the repertoire. Good fun and fellowship and new friendships forged.

Even the birth of my daughter, Karyn, didn't curtail the Guiding activities. In fact, we were never short of baby sitters and Karyn became an honorary Guide from a very early age.

But Guiding in Staffordshire, for me, was not to last. My husband's work necessitated a move to Derbyshire and early in 1970 saw a move further north.

Several return visits were made to Great Haywood over ensuing years and, on one visit, my friend Ann was delighted to be able to tell me that her daughter had just achieved her Queen's Guide Award in the village Guide Company I had started 14 years before. That was a very touching moment for me.

The Derbyshire Rose

So, when Karyn was just nine months old, we settled in Draycott, Derbyshire and the search began for Guide contacts. The wonderful thing about being a Guide member is that you have instant friends wherever you happen to be, and, within no time at all I had met Mary, the Guide Guider in the village. The Guide Company was flourishing. Mary was at the helm and another Guider, whose name I can't recall though I can see her quite clearly, was Mary's irregular assistant. Within a very short space of time, I had become a member of 1st Draycott Guides as Lieutenant.

Although I had been a Captain twice, having a small baby to care for and some teaching commitments too, I was quite happy to take on the supporting role as Mary's assistant. Incidentally, the other Guider, who had appeared occasionally when I first began, left us soon after. I really hope her leaving was nothing to do with my arrival. So, my Guider's hat was now adorned with its third county badge – the Derbyshire Rose.

At my first meeting, it had been suggested that I put Karyn's name down for Brownies. This seemed very strange at the time as she was less than a year old. It proved to be good advice though, as she reached the top of the list only when she became seven years of age – so just the right time. Had I not heeded the advice, I fear she would still be waiting now to become a Brownie. Well, not really, but you know what I mean.

During my first year, in 1970, we celebrated the Diamond Jubilee of the Guide Association.

Metal for Rangers and Guiders

Woven Badge for Brownies and Guides

We readily accepted the 'Three Cheers Challenge' – 'to cheer a person, a place and yourself'. We endeavoured to keep our village of Draycott tidy throughout but don't remember actually having a specific area to tend. We entertained the elderly residents, hoping to cheer them and, of course, we cheered ourselves too, whilst doing so.

Presentation of the Queen's Guide Award to four Draycott Guides
by Long Eaton Division's President. Mary is on the right, I'm on the left.

Change of Direction

After about five years with the Draycott Unit, four of our Senior Guides achieved their Queen's Guide Award. Our numbers continued to grow, as did the waiting list, and Mary managed to persuade me to open a Ranger Unit for those oldest members who were very reluctant to leave Guides. We met in the same place and at the same time as the Guides, meeting in a classroom at Draycott School.

This arrangement worked well and soon we had a very respectable number of Rangers, including several who travelled from Long Eaton and surrounding villages. One of our members was Jane, the daughter of Pat Taft, who later became the Region Chief Commissioner. It has been good to meet up with Pat in subsequent years.

In 1976, we left the village of Draycott and moved to Ockbrook, another village about five miles away. Karyn was mortified as she was approaching her 7th birthday and eagerly awaited her letter form 'Snowy' to say there was a space for her at Brownies. ' If I don't live in Draycott then I won't be able to become a Brownie', she sobbed.

Of course, there was no problem and Karyn's letter duly arrived at our new house, inviting her to become a Draycott Brownie. What excitement there was, for me as well as Karyn. My daughter was to begin her Guiding journey (no Rainbows in those days), and this was such a wonderful feeling and so exciting. I loved taking her to Brownies and peering through the doors at the end of the meeting. Occasionally, I would get asked to do some singing games with them.

Karyn leading her Six through the arch – so she certainly did become a Brownie

Rangers celebrated their Diamond Jubilee in 1977. We were fortunate to have been given sufficient tickets to allow four Draycott Rangers to attend the special celebratory service in St. Pauls' Cathedral. What a magnificent sight greeted us as we entered the cathedral – a sea of aquamarine. I found this quite breathtaking. The service was very special, as was the remainder of the day. We made the almost obligatory visit to CHQ and I invested two members in St. James' Park. For most of them, it was their first visit to London and they were enthralled by the sights and the noisy atmosphere.

What a wonderful day we had

As well as being Ranger Diamond Jubilee, 1977 was also Her Majesty the Queen's Silver Jubilee and she toured the United Kingdom to meet as many young people as she could. Preparations were made for her to come to Derbyshire and there was great excitement amongst the Brownies, Guides and Rangers in Draycott as we had hired a coach to take us to Chatsworth Park, where the Queen was going to meet us all. Karyn decided to cross stitch a celebratory table mat for her and was allowed inside the barrier to present it. The Queen spoke to Karyn and asked if she had made the mat herself. We have a very blurred photograph of 'the presentation' to keep for posterity.

Karyn presenting Her Majesty with the cross stitched mat she had made

I don't remember ever going to camp but we did go each year to Pax Tor, the Brownie House in Darley Dale, near Matlock Bath. This was great fun, especially making bridges over the small stream in the grounds, lighting fires in the large open fireplace in the activity/dining room and, of course, the singing and action songs, initiated by – guess who? Fortunately, I managed to steer clear of the cooking.

Pax Tor

We always had wonderful weekends and both Guides and Guiders looked forward to our annual visit. Pax-Tor is situated on a wooded hillside overlooking the Derwent Valley and was, and still is, an excellent location for walking and exploring the local towns of Matlock and Bakewell. The house was fully equipped for 18 children and 3 adults.

Once a Ranger Guider, I did get together with other Ranger Guiders and we used to meet regularly in the Ranger Bothy in the Derbyshire Dales. We were an assortment of ages and I remember being mesmerised by stories told to us by an elderly Guider who had volunteered for the GIS (Guide International Service), an 'army of goodwill' which helped rebuild a shattered Europe after the Second World War.

This was also the time I was to experience my very first County Training Day after at least 15years of being a Guider. Nowadays, this would be unheard of as training forms an essential part of the leader's qualification and new Guiders (Leaders) are expected to attend a training very early on in their leadership. For me, this training seemed rather a daunting experience as I knew no one else there, but it certainly influenced me in future years when helping to plan County Trainings and when a Trainer myself, I always tried to ensure that trainees did not feel awkward or uneasy, especially if it was their first attendance.

Singing, singing and more singing

It was at this time, in 1978, that I began to work for my Campfire Leader's Certificate. I visited other units to lead their singing for my preliminary sessions and I compiled my box of songs. I had decided to have the songs on separate cards so that I could file them away under different sections and then withdraw and put them in programme order when leading a campfire. I felt this would be easier than having to search through, and carry, a pile of books each time, and it worked really well.

My 'test' had to be undertaken with Guides I didn't know and I had to travel to the other side of Derby to lead the singing at a District event. There seemed so many there but it went well and successfully. I remember planning it around a whirlwind tour to meet Guiding friends around the world. This enabled me to include the requisite songs, games and activities, whilst building it into a musical story.

My Campfire Leader's Badge

Not long after this, I was asked to lead the singing at Glenbrook, the Guide Outdoor Activity Centre in Derbyshire. This was a mixed Guide and Scout event – so quite a challenge. On arrival, I was asked if I needed a microphone and I thought this rather strange. I tend not to be static when leading singing, and use my arms endlessly so I felt that being restricted to a microphone would be too inhibiting. However, it was hard on my vocal cords as my voice tended to disappear before it reached the extremities of those gathered. In future years, and once radio mikes had been invented, I welcomed them with open arms.

After Glenbrook, I was booked to lead the singing at Peak 80, the International Scout and Guide Camp in Chatsworth Park.

Throughout the week, I led the campfire singing in each of the sub-camps. My favourite was leading the German Scouts. They were just fantastic and it was wonderful when they effortlessly harmonised anything on the programme and then serenaded those gathered with songs from their own country.

I was also a regular visitor to Drum Hill, located about 4 miles north of Derby, for campfire singing with the Guides camping there.

I stayed with the Draycott Units for ten years, thoroughly enjoying my time with Mary and the Guides and with the Rangers too. Karyn, by this time, had become a Guide with the 1st Ockbrook Unit. The Guide Hut was about 30 paces away from our back garden gate, down the footpath leading from the Moravian Settlement. This couldn't be more convenient and Karyn really enjoyed her first experiences as a Guide. Her Guider was Penguin, a trainer, so good Guide things were happening. Incidentally, when we moved to Hampshire in future years, we came across a good friend of Penguin's. Jacqui became County Commissioner for Hampshire East.

Peak 80 was Karyn's first Guide Camp. Though she enjoyed it. I fear it was rather overwhelming for her first experience of Guide Camping and she has been a reluctant camper ever since, to the extent that she refused point blank to go when her daughters were Guide age. In fact, my Granddaughters had to rely on Karyn's Brownie friend for camping other than with their Guide Units. Brock would take a week off work to take them each year, ensuring that, for their few days away, they had camped 'properly' as Guides. Good for Brock.

Guiding in Ockbrook

It was whilst at Peak 80 that I was approached by the Commissioner for Ockbrook and Borrowash, asking if I would consider starting a Ranger Unit in Ockbrook. This put me in a rather difficult position as I was still with the Draycott Rangers. I promised to consider it and decided to discuss the situation with Mary. As it happened, a solution was forthcoming as one of my Draycott Rangers was ready for leadership and my departure would enable her to take on this role. Working with Rangers in my own village would be far more convenient for me too as, by this time, I had become the Deputy Head of a school a considerable distance away from home. Not only was this a lengthy journey but there was far more work and responsibility and time was precious.

So, in the Autumn of 1980, the inaugural meeting of the Ockbrook Rangers took place. We made our first public appearance in the village during the Remembrance Day Parade and Service. What a freezing cold and blustery day it was and the Rangers had purchased their aquamarine shirts, navy skirts and hats especially for the parade. They were insistent on not wearing their coats in order to be seen and make an impression. I suppose I could have almost have been seen as being an irresponsible Guider by not ensuring that they wore coats but I didn't want the occasion to be spoilt for them. Fortunately, they all survived the cold and suffered no ill effects.

It was good to be Guiding in the same District as Karyn once more and we were able to share many District events together.

Moving on

Then came the bombshell.

My then husband informed us that he had been offered a job in Hampshire, which obviously necessitated a move south. Karyn announced that she did not want to move schools, having completed her first year at Ockbrook Moravian School, just at the rear of our house.

We moved to Clanfield, just north of Portsmouth, on Royal Wedding Day, 1981 (Prince Charles and Lady Diana Spencer) and Karyn became a boarder at her school, much to my horror. She was able to continue her Guiding in Ockbrook and eventually became a Ranger in the unit I had started.

Time in Clanfield was very short lived as, though I had been fortunate in obtaining a Deputy Headship at Petersgate School in Clanfield, I was soon offered the Headship of Northchapel School, near Petworth in West Sussex. Another move, another Guiding County and another County Badge!

I began Northcahapel School in September, 1982 and quickly discovered that there was a thriving Brownie Pack in the village, run by my infant teacher, Sue, but no Guides. Of course, you can guess what happened. I re-opened Northchapel Guide Company soon after.

'Knowing and Sharing and hoping that always
The Spirit of Guiding will spread the World through'.

Chapter Six

'Today a Commissioner, leading, supporting'

Wonderful Support

There was unbelievable enthusiasm in Northchapel when I mentioned that I would like to re-open the Guide Unit. Canon Wilmer, Chairman of Governors, was the Group Scout Leader. Daph, the School Secretary, was Scout Leader and, of course Sue, my infant teacher, was Brownie Leader. Doris, one of the dinner ladies, had been Brown Owl for many years and her daughter, Ann, had been the Guide Leader until she went to college. I couldn't back out now, even if I'd wanted to.

I dread to think of the initial reaction of the local District Commissioner, Dena, as I began preparations without even consulting her. Sadly, it just hadn't occurred to me that no one in Sussex West Guiding knew me and that I should have liaised with her from the onset. This just went to prove that I was an experienced Guider in one respect and very green in another.

The first Dena knew of the plan was my invitation for her to join us for our initial meeting with the girls and their parents. Whoops! She did give me her approval but not without saying that I should have approached her first. How right she was. I'm sure I was forgiven as Dena and I remain friends to this day and even became President and Vice President of Sussex West Girlguiding together.

1st Northchapel Guides

I started at Northchapel School in the Autumn Term of 1982 and the inaugural meeting of the Guides was held soon after. We began with about eight former Brownies, just sufficient for two patrols. They were very keen and soon had uniforms and were very excited when the unit name tapes eventually arrived. These were sewn on, mostly by mums I'm sure, along with their patrol emblems. Initially, the Guides wanted Patrol names that weren't supplied by CHQ until they realised that they would have to embroider them themselves.

The village hall, where the Scouts and Brownies met, was getting rather tight for spare evenings so meetings in the school seemed an easy and most suitable alternative. This was very convenient for me, especially as, during the Autumn and Spring Terms, I was still travelling from Clanfield.

Once the Summer Term arrived and I was living in the village, it was easier to find places to explore with the Guides. Most Guide nights were spent out of doors, where local woodlands were ideal for building shelters, for tracking and stalking. Outdoor cooking was undertaken in the school grounds. We hadn't yet been able to practice camping skills as we had no equipment, neither had I the necessary qualification to take the Guides camping. However, with several farmer parents, once the Camper's Licence had been acquired and money raised for tentage, there were numerous fields on offer.

My very keen Northchapel Guide, Helen, at her BP Award Presentation

Dounhurst District

Northchapel was part of Dounhurst District with Dena as District Commissioner. We were in Petworth Division with Di as our Division Commissioner. It seemed to be no time at all that I felt really part of my new District and quicker than I had anticipated too. Sue, Brownie Leader, discovered that I enjoyed singing and suggested that we went to the Singing Circle Meeting.

Hazel, the County Campfire Leader, travelled from Worthing to outlying villages, endeavouring to increase the interest in campfire singing in the County. Sue had heard she was going to be in Wisborough Green for Dounhurst members. We arrived and were very impressed with the number of Guiders arriving but, seemingly, no sign of Hazel.

Instead, Dena arrived and began to prepare the room for a meeting. She was pleased to see us and was delighted that we had been able to come to--------------a District Meeting! We had the wrong date for the singing and had made no note of the District Meeting – obviously not planning to attend. We had been there by default but it had been a good opportunity for me to meet others in the District, many of whom I still see today, albeit in Trefoil. I don't believe we ever confessed that we hadn't planned to go!

What a welcome

1983 was flying by and I was quickly made to feel welcome and part of Guiding in Dounhurst District, Petworth Division and Sussex West. There were numerous events for both Guiders and girls so a wonderful opportunity for us all to become really integrated and well established within the County.

There were innumerable trainings, which I found most enjoyable, and these were such a good way of making new friends and, of course, the perfect way to keep up to date with new Guiding initiatives. For some reason, as I have already mentioned, I hadn't attended any Guider trainings whilst in the Midlands, apart from my Ranger gatherings. Maybe they were on offer and I just hadn't taken the opportunity to attend, or maybe it was just before the norm for Guiders to 'Look Wider' and attend. Either way, I missed much.

Dedication of a new County Standard

Sussex West was a newly structured Guide County, having only recently been formed after the reorganization of Sussex into three Guide Counties from two. Consequently, a new County Standard had been lovingly appliqued and embroidered and was now awaiting its dedication. This was to happen in April, 1984, and so early in the New Year, preparations were frantically being made and a choir formed to sing at the Dedication Service which was to take place in the Assembly Hall in Worthing.

Singing and a choir – well, I was there wasn't I – attending each required rehearsal, with Olive as choir leader, assisted by Juliet. Not only was I in my element with the singing but it was so good to meet up with other like-minded Guiders too.

But, I had two 'hiccups' on **the day**!

Firstly, Dena had offered to take me. Karyn was home from school and we were invited to Dena's for lunch prior to our journey to Worthing. I took much time in ensuring that my uniform was immaculate – pressed skirt and blouse, polished shoes, brushed hat and the required colour of tights. Karyn was immaculate too.

We arrived at Dena's. She opened the door and then said, 'you do have your tie don't you.' Horror of horrors, I had omitted to put it on before leaving home. So, a mad dash through the narrow country lanes from Loxwood to Northchapel, and return – with just sufficient time to eat lunch before setting off for Worthing. What a rush and such an embarrassment.

My second 'hiccup' was in the Assembly Hall. I had a very important task to perform – well, not really, but it felt like it. The choir had to process on to the stage onceTthe assembled audience was in place. Members had to remain standing until they were given the signal to 'sit' by me. This was my big moment and I failed. I marched on to the stage and promptly sat down, completely forgetting that I had to gesture with my hand for the choir to be seated before sitting myself. I jumped back up on to my feet and then gave the required signal before sitting down again. Of dear – what a fiasco and how silly I felt.

A festive occasion

Still on the subject of singing, there was to be a County Production at Chichester Festival Theatre, given by the girls and their Guiders just before the Christmas of 1986. The first half comprised of various skits and items whilst the second was the special Carol Service. Juliet gathered together members who wished to form a choir and so Karyn and I, of course, joined in. We spent many, many hours practicing in Christchurch, Chichester, and one of our favourite carols was John Rutter's 'Star Carol'.

The big day came – what organisation and excitement. Marquees had to be erected for dressing rooms as the theatre's were not 'man enough' to hold all participants. Walkie Talkie sets had to be mastered for efficient communication between stage and dressing rooms. Instructions were given for the 'dress code' – even down to the colour of our tights, which had to be purchased from M&S!

Tickets were at a premium and the theatre was full to overflowing. The first half came and went – enjoyed by all. The ceremony of the presentation of flags and standards followed before the Carol Service began. It was magical. Our voices were tuned and Juliet looked pleased, and a little relieved.

Then came the 'Star Carol'. Juliet had given us strict instructions to follow her 'to the letter', which of course we did, even to the point of not coming in when we knew we should, as Juliet hadn't indicated to us. And so it was that we missed out an entire verse of the Star Carol, but we carried it off with such aplomb that I'm sure there were none in the audience who actually realised.

Not disillusioned

Despite my portrayal of a seemingly 'dulally' Guider at the Dedication of the County Standard, Dena asked me, soon after, to become her Assistant District Commissioner – a warranted appointment then. I was delighted and readily accepted. It was good to work more closely with her and assist in the numerous District events and activities.

This appointment lasted for a year and then I received a telephone call from Division Commissioner, Di, who explained that the Division Executive had decided to form a new District, of which Northchapel would form apart. As for the new District Commissioner, it was to be me, if I was interested. Of course I was, and, once I had gained approval from Penny, our County Commissioner, I joined Dena and the other District Commissioners of Petworth Division on the Division team, as District Commissioner for the new Leconfield District. Leconfield was chosen as many of our members lived and worked within the Leconfield Estate of Petworth House. I had to seek permission from Lord Leconfield and this was readily given.

Petworth Park

Numbers in our Guide Unit were rising and we joined in readily with District and Division activities and the joint Scout/Guide Camp in Petworth Park held over the May Day weekend each year. It was at this camp that I really came to discover the differences between camping as a Guide and camping as a Scout. No such things as bedding racks in Scout tents, nor bedding rolls but Scouts certainly knew how to make large structures such as gates to mark entry to their camps and obstacle courses.

One year, Daph and I decided to try the obstacle course. I do not like heights so was very unsure about climbing over the wooden wall. However, Peter, the Billingshurst Scout Commissioner, came to my rescue and helped me round. Peter and I continue to meet yearly at Sussex West Trefoil's Friendship Service.

A Gang Show

We were very much a 'family group' too, with the Brownies, Cubs, Scouts, Guides and Venture Scouts really supporting each other and the village. Daph and I decided to put on a Gang Show and many hours were spent compiling items, seeking help from Peter in Billingshurst, finding music, practicing and finally performing. Daph was the producer and I the Musical Director. What fun we had and such tremendous support was given by parents and villagers.

Daph is on the left of the front standing row, I'm on the extreme right of this row.

Karyn is with her Venture Scout friends, back row – 3rd from right

A dilemma

Leaders in the District remained fairly constant but, as District Commissioner, I was given the almost impossible task of finding a replacement 'Brown Owl' for Northchapel Brownies. Sue was imminently expecting her first child and decided to leave Brownies once she had left her teaching appointment. There was just no one to take the Brownies – a thriving and full pack – but it just couldn't close.

A solution was at hand. Sheila, a friend and a Guide Guider, agreed to take over Guides and I took up the challenge of leading a Brownie Pack. Northchapel Brownies were used to having annual pack holidays so I prepared to take my Pack Holiday LIcence alongside my Music in the Pack certificate. Within a year I was a fully fledged Brown Owl, to add to my experience of working with Rangers and Guides.

Switzerland and 'Our Chalet'

One of my first invitations as District Commissioner was to Wisborough Green Guides to present an award and also lead the campfire singing. It was at this meeting that I met Carol, who had taken groups of Guides to Switzerland on numerous occasions. We chatted and I asked if Karyn and I might be included in her next expedition.

This was to be the first of so many visits , initially every two years, and eventually every year, staying first in Adelboden, close to 'Our Chalet' and latterly in Grindelwald. I just loved the country, the hikes, the mountains and the people. I was hooked.

My first visit was in 1985 and I eventually visited eleven times with Guides, alternate years assisting Carol, alternate years leading groups from Cornwall. Then, with Karyn for Thinking Day 1995 and my granddaughters in 2011 when Abiee renewed her Promise at 'Our Chalet'. I introduced my Trefoil Friend, Eunice, to Switzerland and 'Our Chalet' in 2018. Hopefully, there will still be more visits to come.

Ready to leave for Switzerland
Left to right: Karyn, me, Sheila

In 1992, my group from Cornwall was staying in Bonderlen, just a short walk up the hill from 'Our Chalet'. We always tried to be in Switzerland for Swiss National Day on August 1st and I realised that our proposed trip would also coincide with the 60th birthday of 'Our Chalet'.

We were able to join in those wonderful celebrations alongside members from all over the World. What a truly magnificent occasion – from the Market Place, to the Pageant, the presentation of the large wooden trefoil to 'Our Chalet' by Robert Trummer-Ryf, the woodcarver, the singing led by Marion and the wonderful and emotional moment when, unbeknown to everyone, a local 'friend' of 'Our Chalet', who had been secretly practicing 'The Chalet Song' on his alpine horn, accompanied us as we stood around the flagpole.

The most magical moment for Karyn and I was the singing of the World Song – all members singing in their own languages, surrounded by those wonderful mountains with 'our Chalet' in the background, and accompanied by the alpine horn. Words cannot describe the emotion we felt.

A real mountain top moment – with Graffham Guides at the top of the First, overlooking Grindelwald, before its glacier almost melted away in subsequent years

All Change

I enjoyed several happy years in Sussex West in various roles, which I will enlarge upon in my next chapter, before my work took me to Cornwall for a time. I handed over the District to Hazel and headed west.

The beginning of a new era

This was April, 1989, and I had arrived in Seaton, Cornwall (not to be confused with Seaton in Devon). I moved in to my bungalow, which was up a very steep and unmade lane, giving it glorious views of the sea and the Eddystone Lighthouse – which, incidentally, flashed twice every six seconds.

I was looking forward to Guiding in a new area and had already received a wonderful welcoming letter from Angela, Cornwall's County Training Adviser. She had been visiting Foxlease a week after I had visited and Chris, Assistant Guider in Charge, had explained to her that I was leaving Sussex and moving to Cornwall.

It was at this time that my belief in the true spirit of Guiding became even more apparent. I learned that my husband of nearly 25 years was 'trading me in for a younger model'. I was in a new house, new area, new headship, on my own and knew no one. But, of course, that wasn't true was it. I 'knew' my Guiding family and, though they didn't know, initially, of my marriage traumas, I found that I had so many instant friends and it was this 'true spirit of Guiding' that helped me through those difficult days.

Further Challenges

My new Headship was at St. Dunstan's Abbey Preparatory School in Plymouth. I commuted from Cornwall to Devon each day, crossing the Tamar Bridge and occasionally taking the Tamar Ferry.

I quickly realised that many of my girls had tremendously long journeys to and from school each day and therefore arrived home too late to attend Rainbows or Brownies in their own localities. What could I do to help? The answer was simple – open units at school. So, the 19th Devonport Rainbows and Brownies came into being and I became 'Sunshine' and 'Brown Owl'. I had, by now, discovered the world of a Rainbow – a section I had initially been so against. As a teacher, I knew how tired children were at the end of the school day and I just felt that children of rainbow age would be so much better staying at home with mum at the end of a school day. Thank goodness I was proved wrong. I quickly realized what a wonderful opportunity it was for girls of Rainbow age to start on their wonderful Guiding journey.

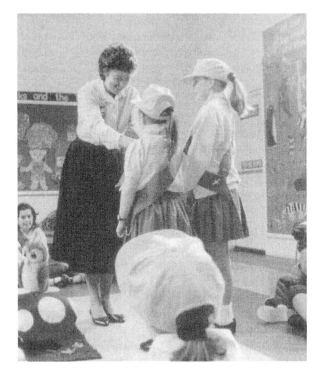

With my St. Dunstan's Abbey Brownies. Catherine had just presented Clare to me to make her Promise as a Brownie.

I was now actively Guiding in two counties at the same time as, not long after my move to Seaton, I was asked to become District Commissioner for St. German's District, of which Seaton formed part.

I enjoyed being part of the Division Team of Caradon, with Margaret at the helm, and was thrilled when she asked me to become her Assistant Division Commissioner. This was such a wonderful opportunity to experience Guiding throughout Cornwall, and not just on my local patch.

I had already made many 'singing' friends as I very quickly discovered, and joined, Kernow Singing Circle. This necessitated many miles of travel each month as we journeyed to the different meeting places throughout the county, wearing our canary yellow sweatshirts. I really don't think we sang as sweetly as canaries though! What a good opportunity to get to know the highways and byways of Cornwall whilst enjoying the singing of songs old and new, under the leadership of Ali.

Caradon's Division Commissioner's term of office came to an end in October 1991 and I felt privileged to be asked by Angela, who by now, had become County

Commissioner, to take over from Margaret. I handed the reins of St. German's District to Rita and took up my next Guiding challenge. The few years in my new role were tremendously rewarding and enjoyable and I found Cornwall Guiding to be vibrant and exciting.

Busy, busy, busy

I just loved my role as Division Commissioner. I had a wonderful team – one that contributed ideas, with members working well together to put those ideas into practice. We had many Division functions, including a day at Dobwalls Theme Park, now no longer in existence, camps and training days for girls as well as Guiders, competitions, patrol leaders' weekends, Brownie and Rainbow days and many more. What fun I had and I hope the girls did too. They certainly supported all events.

New Standards

A large sum of money had been bequeathed to Cornwall Guiding and it was decided to use the money to replace the very old Division Standards. Much planning and preparation went into the design and making of these and, in Caradon, we tried to ensure that all who wished were able to add a stitch or two.

My responsibility was to stitch the words 'Caradon' and 'Be Prepared'. It was quite a thought that our contributions would travel on in time for future Guiding in Cornwall.

Margaret, past Division Commissioner, and I with the new standard. I was pleased with 'my wording'.

Once all the standards were complete, a Service of Dedication was held in Truro Cathedral. What a magnificent occasion this was and I felt tremendously proud to follow 'my Standard' as it was processed up the aisle by my good (and very sadly missed) friend Brenda, who had overseen the making of it, and Jan, a fellow escapee from Sussex and now a District Commissioner in our Division.

Brenda and I were in the choir and we had many hours of fun whilst learning the anthems, descants and alto parts of the music, under the direction of Julie and Ali. The new Standards were resplendent, as was the occasion – and one certainly never to be forgotten.

All but one of Cornwall's Division Commissioners waiting for the Dedication Service to begin. I guess the missing one took the photo!

It is said that 'a change is as good as a rest'

It was in October 1994, I learned that my Headship at St. Dunstan's Abbey Preparatory School was to come to an end. The Governors had decided, for financial reasons, to merge the Senior and Preparatory Schools under the leadership of just one head, which was to be the head of the Senior School.

I was to leave at the end of the Autumn Term. What a shock, but, undeterred, I resolved to move back to Sussex to be closer to Karyn, who was by now married to Ian, and living and teaching in Hampshire.

So, in January, 1995, I bade farewell to Cornwall, and Devon, and returned to Sussex. I had experienced the warmth and friendship of Cornish Guiding and had learned so much. I would miss my Cornish Guiding friends greatly.

I obtained temporary teaching appointments for the Spring and Sumer terms in Sussex before becoming a lecturer in Early Childhood Education at Chichester College. This was a change of direction but one I relished and thoroughly enjoyed.

Sussex West Guiding again – with a bit of Hampshire too!

It didn't take me long to be reintegrated into Sussex West Guiding. Juliet, County Music Adviser, had hoped I would become County Campfire Leader again, one of the roles I had prior to my move to Cornwall. However, Mags, County Commissioner, had other ideas and so it was that I became County Training Adviser, working closely with my good friend Margaret, who was County Training Chairman.

I still wanted a unit appointment and so Karyn and I decided to work together in Hampshire and open a Rainbow Unit in Waterlooville, where Karyn was living. She was the leader and I her assistant. I was so proud of her with her original ideas and superb rapport with the girls, and I loved those few years working together. Sadly, once Abiee arrived, Karyn decided to withdraw from active Guiding so I decided to work with a Rainbow Unit in Chichester instead. This was conveniently situated close to college and I was allowed to leave work early to arrive at the meetings in time.

What me?

It was good to be back in Sussex and, in no time at all it seemed I had never been away. I enjoyed my various Guiding roles in the three years I had been back but I was not prepared for the next one I was offered.

In May, 1998, Mag's term of office as County Commissioner came to an end. I knew that Division Commissioners had been asked by Region to suggest who they felt would be an ideal successor but I had no idea that the person nominated would be me.

In December, 1997, Frances, Region Chief Commissioner, telephoned to invite me to become the next County Commissioner for Sussex West. What a daunting thought. I was to follow in the footsteps of Olave, Lady Baden-Powell, who had been the first County Commissioner for Sussex.

I readily accepted the challenge and it was a very special moment when I renewed my Promise as the new County Commissioner for Sussex West.

At least I have my mouth shut in the press release photo above – which is most unusual – unlike the one below, taken outside Chichester Cathedral before a County Thinking Day Service!!

I had the time of my life, touring around the County, visiting, helping and supporting the girls and their leaders.

Here I am, helping Rainbows sing their new song at a County AGM

Being looked after at a Division Camp.

Not just one coffee, but two!!

'Working together' outside the barn at a County Weekend at Foxlease

Rewarding times

What enormous fun I had in carrying out my new role and what tremendous responsibility I felt. My few years as CC were just fantastic. I loved being invited to the many and various activities undertaken and to meeting the girls and their Leaders, and all the other adults too.

I felt so proud of everyone, who were doing their best to maximise all Guiding opportunities, whilst having such tremendous fun themselves and learning all those relevant and important skills. What a team I had – all striving to ensure that Sussex West Guiding was going from strength to strength. I felt enormously privileged.

The 'fly in the ointment'

Penny, retired County Commissioner and County President, referred to Ron as the 'fly in the ointment'. If that was the case, then Ron is the best 'fly' I have ever known.

I hadn't planned to remarry but along came Ron, a retired Fireman, who swept me off my feet and asked for 'my hand in marriage'. I said 'yes', though I knew that being County Commissioner wasn't conducive to newly married life with a husband who had never experienced Guiding or Scouting. As a result, and after much soul searching and considerable regret, I decided to relinquish the role of County Commissioner before my term of office expired. I know this was the right decision but it was a very hard one to make.

And so it was that, in May 2000, I handed over to Rachel and wished her and the County 'good luck' and ''God speed' for their future Guiding.

'Whatever the challenge, decision or outcome,
I'll never forget I'm a Guide through and through'

Chapter Seven

'Today an Adviser, helping our Leaders
Provide for the girls in that great Guiding way'

Let me take you back to the 1980s in Sussex West. I was fairly new to the County and had just been appointed as District Commissioner for Leconfield.

The picture below shows me receiving the 'Flame of Friendship' in 1985 to mark the occasion of Guiding's 75th Anniversary. The flame had to travel by land, water and air. The County flame had arrived by helicopter and landed at Goodwood Race course. For Dounhurst District, it travelled by land to Petworth Park where it was handed over to District Commissioners to share with their members – travelling over water. I believe we used the lake in Petworth Park. The flame is being handed to me by Di, Division Commissioner.

Singing, Singing ------------

Sue and I always tried to go to Hazel's Singing Circle meetings when they were held in Petworth and often I would travel beyond the Division too. Hazel persuaded me to join the London Guiders' Singing Group and this was great fun. We travelled to Victoria together for the Saturday meetings and I quickly got to know fellow members from around the Region and beyond. Initially, meetings were held at CHQ and we would have our coffee and lunch in its restaurant. Later, when CHQ was being remodeled, the venue changed. We had several, but all within the vicinity of Victoria, ranging from various Church Halls, sometimes at Westminster Cathedral and at the Westminster City School in Bressenden Place.

It was at this school that we made our recordings for the tapes, under the leadership of Hettie Smith. What a wonderful person she was, always ensuring that our enunciation was beyond reproach, and the dynamics too.

We would make a perfect rendition of a song only to be told, by the sound technician, that an underground train had rumbled by and we would have to sing it again. The words and tunes of those early songs will stay with me forever.

> *'And were you a Brownie, and did you delight*
> *To dress up in uniform shining and bright'*

Karyn and I so enjoyed that experience and the camaraderie of our fellow members.

An invitation

Sometime during this period, County Commissioner, Penny asked if I would like to attend a music training at Foxlease along with Juliet, our County Music Adviser. Each County had been offered two places. I felt very honoured to have been asked and, of course, I readily accepted.

The weekend duly arrived and I set off with Juliet on the appointed Friday, as soon as we had both finished our teaching commitments. I had some trepidation, for two reasons. This was the first time I had returned to Foxlease since being 'locked out' as a Ranger, and it was a Music Training!

Now, although I loved singing and leading campfires, I did not consider myself a music specialist. I was fearful that I wouldn't cope. Juliet, bless her, realised my predicament and was so supportive and helpful, especially when some music expertise was needed. I had a wonderful time and had many reasons to be thankful. I had returned to Foxlease, just loving the atmosphere and surroundings, and I had met Margaret Venables, the CHQ Music Consultant. We very quickly became friends and, until a few years ago, were still in touch.

In fact, it was Margaret who enabled me to have a 'Mountain Top Moment' as, when she retired, she asked me to help her lead the singing in Westminster Abbey on 23rd February, 1991, for the Thinking Day Service. My position was in the choirstalls with the dignitaries. I had to keep an eye on Margaret who was conducting the main body of the Abbey and then keep the invited guests in time with everyone else. I had great difficulty in getting them to sing at first but then decided, rightly or wrongly, to make it a competition between the two sides. First, I managed to get one side singing, then encouraged the other side to do better. It worked!!! It was a brilliant weekend, all expenses paid, and certainly worth travelling from Cornwall on the Friday, for the rehearsal, and then the service on Saturday morning – and purchasing the very recently launched Geoff Banks 'new uniform'. Such great fun and a moving service.

------------- **and more singing**

I was already leading many campfires around Sussex West, including the County Days that Hazel had been unable to attend, and the Saturday evening singing at several residential trainings. During the 75th Celebrations at Goodwood in 1985, when the 'flame of Guiding' arrived by helicopter, Penny asked me to assist.

Hazel was leading the singing with the Brownies, Guides, Rangers and Guiders outside in the grandstand whilst, inside, my task was to lead the dignitaries and Division representatives in the singing of the specially written anniversary song, 'Let's take hands in friendship'. No problem, I thought. I knew the song and had no trouble pitching but when the moment came to begin, all I could hear coming from outside was the sound of hundreds of girls singing at the tops of their voices, 'whoops came the marmalade and whoops came the jam'!!!!!!! I found it very hard to put on my 'serious face'. A challenge indeed, but such good fun.

Getting ready to lead the dignitaries in the singing.
Only Jo and I seemed to see the funny side of the proceedings!

County Campfire Singing Adviser

As time went on, Penny asked me if I would consider taking on the role of County Campfire Singing Adviser. Hazel's appointment had come to an end and a successor was needed. Now I just couldn't refuse, could I, and my appointment commenced in September 1988. This role was 'right up my street' and I relished the opportunity of furthering Hazel's sterling work.

It was at this time that I became a member of Foxlease Singing Circle, not attending the weekends but the monthly evening meetings. These were held in 'Scotland' at Foxlease, usually led by Pat. We would have a wonderful sing, break for hot chocolate and then more singing. There were never many of us but we were able to sing in several parts. Karyn and I learned many wonderful songs – some that could be shared generally with Guiders and girls and some just for our pure enjoyment.

It was only when I moved to Cornwall that I began to attend the weekend singing sessions with Brenda and several other Cornish Guiders. At that time Ali, our Kernow Singing Circle Leader, was not a member of FSC so it was a lovely surprise when, after a gap of several years after my remarriage, I found Ali to be, not only a member but secretary too.

Encouraging

Most County Days would find me taking campfire singing sessions, sometimes general and sometimes more specialist for Guides or Brownies, or singing games for 'for the non musical'. I was able to encourage Guiders to work towards their 'Campfire Leader' or 'Music in the Pack' certificates. Evenings and weekends would find me travelling to Blacklands and other campsites, to unit meetings or District and Division events or County Residential Trainings.

I remember travelling back from Blacklands with Sheila one evening, after leading a session at a County Camp. We absolutely reeked of wood smoke and I was very hoarse. As we approached the village of Anstey, we were stopped by a Police Patrol car. 'Have you been drinking Madam?', was the question asked. 'Only cocoa', I replied. Initially, our interceptor was not amused, but he looked at us both, saw our attire and probably had a whiff of our strange aroma before smiling and indicated for us to 'go on our way'.

I just loved my role but this was to be short lived as my move to Cornwall took place in April 1989. I had completed just eight months. Sadly, I was the last Campfire Singing Adviser in Sussex West; no-one else was ever appointed. Thank goodness Juliet continues, to this day, to be Music Consultant.

___

On the move again

So, Cornwall, here I come. It didn't take me long 'to find my singing feet' there. Ali made Brenda and I very welcome at the monthly Kernow Singing Circle meetings and, for a time, when Ali had moved away, I coordinated the group.

Not long after my arrival in the County, I volunteered to help Sue with 'Music in the Pack' and 'Campfire Leader's' trainings at a County Arts Day. I was just going to be her 'gofer' – no bigger role. On the Friday evening, I received a phone call from Sue to say she was unwell and would be unable to take the trainings. So, with hasty, last minute planning, I took these trainings myself and what a wonderful way it was of becoming integrated into my new County. As it happened, Sheila from Sussex, had come to stay for the weekend and so she became my 'gofer'. Again, I was in my element, doing something I really enjoyed.

That day, at Penrice School, was the start of many 'singing sessions' taken throughout the County, the most memorable being the Saturday evening campfires in the ballroom of the Bay Hotel in Newquay – the venue for the annual residential County Weekend Trainings.

I tried to create a balance between sensible songs and more lively ones, including action songs and singing games. These evenings were always 'organised' but did become very raucous and noisy. I never lost control - not quite anyway – but they were always such fun. I remember Jane Lewis, a CHQ trainer, saying that we were all completely mad in Cornwall but how much she enjoyed coming.

It was Jane that made a paper duck when we were all doing the actions to

> *'Oh wasn't it a bit of luck that I was born a baby duck'*

I'm not sure how she managed it – but once we had all returned to our places, that paper duck seemed to waddle across the floor!

County Rainbow Adviser

It was in Cornwall that I realised the relevance of the Rainbow Section. I have already mentioned earlier how, initially, I was so against Rainbows, but the more I worked with them, the more I began to realise their importance.

Having been in Cornwall for four years, I was asked by Angela, County Commissioner, if I would consider becoming County Rainbow Adviser. I could not refuse, could I? I enjoyed working with the Rainbow age group and I felt it a great privilege to be able to start them on their wonderful Guiding journey. So, in April 1993, my appointment was ratified.

I loved supporting and encouraging the Rainbow Guiders and enthusing others who were as skeptical as I had been.

The original Rainbow Promise Badge was a triangular cloth badge, featuring a Rainbow under a Guide Badge. It was sewn against the neckline of the tabard, with the upper point of the triangle meant to touch against the binding on the top edge of the tabard.

It was good to meet Rainbow Advisers from around the Region and further afield too. We had many Region get-togethers, with Virginia, our Region Adviser, including several residential weekends. Here we planned resources as, at that time, those for Rainbows were very limited. A Rainbow Recipe Book was suggested along with a Rainbow Prayer Book. Contributions were requested from all counties in the Region and our weekends were spent in collating these ready for distribution.

I had the opportunity to attend many trainings, including those at Foxlease and even Netherud in Scotland. Wendy Jarvis, CHQ Rainbow Adviser, was the lead trainer and we were to meet on so many occasions in the future. Coincidently, Wendy was Headteacher of Eglinton Road Infant School in Plumstead, London. I had attended Eglinton Road Junior School as a child, where Miss Johnson had been my teacher and also a Brown Owl – the one I had pestered when a Brownie at the Jamboree all those years previously.

'Playing' at Netherud with Olive supervising!!

County Training Adviser

I returned to Sussex West in January 1995 and by March 1995 I had become County Training Adviser, working with Margaret, who was County Training Chairman. No wonder Mags hadn't heeded Juliet's request for me to return to my previous role as Campfire Singing Adviser. She obviously had other plans for me.

Margaret and I worked well together and planned many a training, both day and residential. We travelled together to Region meetings in London and took every opportunity to keep up to date with new initiatives so that our Guiders delivered the programme to their girls in the best way possible, and Commissioners managed and led their teams effectively. Venues for residentials included Dunford House near Midhurst, Foxlease in Hampshire, Lodge Hill near Pulborough and Great Haubois House in Norfolk. These were always well received and enormous fun.

It had always been the tradition, at residential trainings, for the Chairman and Adviser to deliver the early morning tea to residents' bedrooms. Now, I am NOT a morning person and I found this incredibly difficult, especially as I always looked forward to a lie-in at weekends, after my early mornings during the week for work. There were a few times that I let Margaret down, sadly, as I didn't wake up in time, but I knew (hope) she understood.

We had some strong personalities in our small training team and this proved quite a challenge when trying to recruit new trainers and ensure that views and needs of all trainers were heeded. However, we had much fun in our team activities, particularly at the Annual Trainers' Camp in Finch's garden.

How well I remember Sue sitting on a hay bale, holding forth on some subject or other, and then tipping backwards, landing on her shoulders with feet in the air, skirt wrapped around her head and wine glass still intact! What a sight – and the tears of laughter just flowed.

Christmas meals were always splendid affairs too, with our own 'resident chef', Sue, being a wonderful hostess. She never ceased to amaze us with her culinary skills and looked after us so well. With plentiful food, flowing wine, silly hats and cracker jokes, who could fail to enjoy these evenings.

I know my place!

Whilst I was Training Adviser, the County took over the Connaught Theatre in Worthing for another County Production, produced by Joan, with Juliet as Musical Director. As there were so many girls involved, and their guiders too, it soon became apparent that more loos would be needed. So, 'Portaloos' to the rescue.

These were positioned in the car park adjacent to the theatre and someone was needed to 'man' these loos and deter members of the public from using them. Now, who has always had a reputation for frequently needing the loo, and who gives directions, not by Public Houses but by loos. Well, me of course. And who was given this very important task and very unique role – that of 'loo attendant'? It just had to be me, didn't it! Need I say more, except to say that somewhere I have a photograph to prove it!

Foxlease

It was at about this time I was invited to become a member of Foxlease Management Committee, initially with Gill Campbell as Chairman. Gill was eventually succeeded by Stella Goldsmith.

It was a great privilege to serve on this committee and I really enjoyed the involvement in the financial aspects of the house, and having a major hand in future initiatives of this important training centre. I found it fascinating and so enlightening.

My time on the committee coincided with a visit from Princess Margaret. Now that was very special, being able to talk, and take tea, with her in the dining room. Had it really been all those years since I was giving out litter bags and selling programmes as a Ranger in Parliament Square on her Wedding Day?

Another Role

I derived a huge amount of pleasure and satisfaction in my Adviser roles. I thoroughly enjoyed the contact with Guiders and Commissioners, both within the County and beyond, whilst not losing touch with the girls. After all, there would be no future for Guiding if it wasn't for the girls. We must nurture them and steer them forward in their Guiding so they too can make a difference to themselves and the world.

It was, therefore, another 'Mountain Top Moment' for me when I was asked to take on the role of County Commissioner and renewed my Promise as I embarked on this exciting new journey.

> **'Embracing new trends and initiatives gladly.**
> **Upholding that vision of times far away.'**

Chapter Eight

'Today I'm a Trainer, enthusing our members, Enhancing their skills for our 'girls in the lead'

I refused 'point blank' to become a trainer. That was the middle of the 80s in Sussex West and Dena suggested I might like to consider this option. 'No way', I said. 'I teach during the day and have no wish to do so in my leisure time'.

So, what changed my mind?

It was whilst I was in Cornwall as Rainbow Adviser; I was spending more and more time taking sessions at County Days for Rainbow Guiders, interspersed with running singing and music sessions. I realised that this was totally different to the teaching I was doing during the day, and so decided that I may as well take my trainer's qualification, as I had nothing to lose and much to gain. I just loved enthusing adult leaders in their work with the girls,

The process begins --

I had to be recommended by County to Region and, once accepted, was assigned a tutor and put in a group with other prospective trainers. There were four of us in our tutor group, under the watchful eye of Anneleise. Two of us were from Cornwall and two from Devon. We met in Plymouth.

What we were unaware of, initially, was that our group had been 'turned down' by several other tutors in the Region – perhaps we appeared a little daunting to take on. We were all very experienced Guiders and all with County Appointments. How well we worked together, though, and Anneleise was fantastic whilst she put us stringently through our paces. We had so many tasks to prepare and present at our monthly meetings and worked extremely hard in the process. The camaraderie was fantastic and we gave each other such wonderful support too.

-   and the process ends

It seemed no time at all that we had completed all the necessary criteria, including observation of sessions undertaken. You would think that, for experienced teachers, of which there were two, this would not faze us. However, we were most anxious to ensure that our aims and objectives were appropriate and that they were met by the end of the sessions, and this caused a great deal of stress and anxiety. I suppose we felt that our teaching capabilities were under scrutiny too.

The award of our Training Licences

We were all extremely relieved once we knew that we had 'passed', and we were ecstatic. All that hard work had been well worth the effort and we were let loose on Guiders in other Counties, as well as our own.

I just loved travelling around the Region and meeting other Trainers and Guiders. My 'training years' were so fulfilling.

I have happy memories of training in Somerset, Dorset, Devon and Hampshire at that time – to name but a few. I remember training in Somerset on a particular occasion when I set my trainees a task to undertake in the grounds of the school. The environment, I felt, was often under used by Rainbows, at that time, but made a perfect area for 'exploring and discovering' – one of the eight points of the Rainbow programme.

I sent my trainees off into the grounds and began chatting to the County Chairman of Training, Ruth. She seemed amazed that I had dispatched my group and told me that mine was the first Rainbow group she had come across that had been set a task outside their designated training room. I found this so hard to believe but was soon to realise that this was indeed true, at that time as, wherever I trained subsequently, I found out from the trainees that this really was the case. I have always firmly believed in utilising all resources.

Training in Cornwall

There were so many opportunities to train in Cornwall and it was here that I learned the term 'Half County Day'. When I first arrived, I just could not get my head around what was being referred to when this term was used. However, all was revealed in the fullness of time.

Cornwall, as you will be aware, is a very long and narrow County and trainees from Lands End could not be expected to travel to my Division of Caradon, close to the River Tamar and bordering Devon. So, Half County Trainings were held and sessions duplicated in the east and the west of the County. This proved to be a really good experience for me, a new trainer, as I quickly learned that, though the title of the training might be the same, the delivery would depend on the trainees themselves. Of course, I knew this from my 'day job' working with children but I hadn't appreciated that it was the same for adults too.

Distracting views

Each year, Cornwall held a residential training weekend in the Bay Hotel in Newquay and this was a perfect venue – though distracting.

For several years I took sessions for the Rainbow Guiders and these were always held in the bar of the hotel. Now you might think that it was the alcohol that was the distraction – but it was the view!!

I decided to organise 'my room' so that the trainees had their backs to the sea view to lessen the distraction. There were always many surfers performing intricate tricks upon the waves.

This worked really well until I found **my** eyes focusing on the antics of a particular surfer. How long I watched and whether my trainees realised, I do not know, but, having realised myself, I had to be really firm with myself to concentrate on the matter in hand.

An elevating experience

One evening, after school, I received a telephone call from Angela, Cornwall's County Commissioner, asking me if I would be willing to travel to the Isles of Scilly to take a training for the Rainbow and Brownie Guiders. It definitely had to be accepted.

A date was agreed and I tried to book my flight. I really fancied travelling in the helicopter as this would have been a new experience. Sadly, though, all flights were full. The only other option open to me was the small plane departing from the vicinity of Penzance. Luggage was limited so I had to ensure that my training resources fitted in to a very small suitcase. Runways at both ends were grass and the maximum number of passengers was six.

Skybus To The Scillies

What spectacular views of the Scilly Isles as we approached – truly a bird's eye view.

The appointed day arrived and I set off bright and early, having spent the night with the local Division Commissioner. I caught the first flight out, which left at the crack of dawn, and landed at St. Mary's at 9.30 am ready for a 10.00am start. It was planned to have sessions in the morning and afternoon with breaks for coffee, lunch and tea.

The District Commissioner, when she realised that this was my first visit, juggled the times of the sessions, so that we worked through our coffee break and had a late lunch to finish the day. This meant that there would be time to give me a whistle stop tour of the island before catching the last flight back to the mainland.

It was great to meet the Guiders and they were so appreciative of a visit from a 'mainlander'. I was made so welcome and it seemed like a trip back in time. Houses were never locked, nor were cars, and crime hardly existed. The inhabitants were so friendly. Simply magnificent views from every corner led me to fall in love with the island and I vowed to return. This I have done, visiting from cruise ships when the Isles of Scilly have been on the itinerary.

Foxlease

I loved my training experiences in the South West and hoped, when I eventually moved back to Sussex, that I would still keep a link with this region.

Anneleise was instrumental in linking me with Foxlease as a Trainer. Her Division weekend was my first training experience there, the title being, 'Towards the Millennium'. This was the start of many Foxlease trainings, which always felt very special, and a far cry from my first visit when I was 'locked out'.

It was at Foxlease, whilst taking a group of Rainbow Guiders one weekend, that I had a rather embarrassing experience. I always incorporated some singing into my sessions and this particular weekend coincided with the recent launch of 'The Anglia Rainbow Collection'. I learnt one of the songs and proceeded to teach it to my group. It went well and seemed to be enjoyed. I explained that it was new to me and I hoped the tune was correct. One of the trainees put my mind at rest and assured me that the tune was absolutely correct. A little surprised, I asked her if she had sung it before. 'Oh yes', she said. 'I wrote it' !!!!!

Back to Sussex

I trained whenever I could, either in the County, or beyond, and it was good to meet so many Guiders and other trainers too. Training for me was so rewarding and I felt I was 'doing my bit' to give a little back to Guiding. I owed so much to Guiding. It had helped me enormously and I had so much to be grateful for, right from my earliest days as a Brownie.

Training, I felt, enabled me to help Guiding go from strength to strength so that the girls, through their Guiders, truly maximised all opportunities to enable them to be the best they could be and help them develop into active, caring and involved women.

Working as County Training Adviser with Margaret, County Training Chairman, was great. We had such fun organising trainings within the County, which included residentials as well as days and evenings.

I had attended trainings in all the Guide Centres, except Lorne, though I have now visited when in Ireland for a National Trefoil Annual Meeting. I was fortunate to train Durham South County at Waddow, almost needing an interpretor!! There is something really special about training in the Guide Centres (now called TACS – Training and Activity Centres).

Further embarrassment

Whilst in Sussex, I was asked by Wendy, CHQ Rainbow Adviser, if I would be the trainer for her County's residential training in Kent. I agreed but was slightly concerned about training with **the** CHQ specialist in the group. However, I planned my weekend's programme and was confident that I would deliver balanced and appropriate sessions.

My aims and objectives were clearly defined, my resources collected and my boxes packed, ready for my journey to Cranbrook. Rainbow Rabbit was sitting on the top of one of my boxes. Rainbow Rabbit was introduced, to help the Rainbows with remembering to keep their Promise, and the soft-toy version with her felt tabard was adopted as a mascot by many units.

What I had failed to appreciate was that Wendy did not like Rainbow Rabbit. This character had been introduced to the section without her involvement and she just **hated**, emphatically **hated**, this creature.

I arrived at the centre for the weekend, with said Rabbit, and was greeted by Wendy with the words, 'Oh no – I'm not having that ---------- rabbit here'. Well, I was actually lost for words, albeit for just a very short time. Those who know me will appreciate that I can't stay quiet for long. However, I didn't feel that I could go against Wendy's wishes, being the ultimate 'Rainbow Lady' in the Country, so Rainbow Rabbit was confined to my bedroom and my programme hastily altered so that the ------------rabbit was not referred to or used. This didn't bode well for the weekend. And, I happened to like Rainbow Rabbit.

Also, unbeknown to me, there were rumblings in the County about some of the County Personnel, who happened to be at the training that weekend. Sparks were flying and this did not make for a happy weekend. I had my work cut out trying to ensure that the Rainbow Guiders did not get too embroiled in this unhappy atmosphere. How sad I felt that Guiding was not as perfect as it should have been.

The evaluations reassured me that I had achieved what I set out to do, but I was reminded, during that weekend, of those two CA sisters, when I was a Guide, who made my Guiding life very difficult for a time. Sadly, there can be problems in all walks of life, even within Guiding. I later learned that Wendy, shortly after, had joined a neighbouring County, so hopefully a happy ending.

Commissioner Training, Tutoring and Mentoring

It wasn't long before I was asked to train Commissioners within our County, and in neighbouring Counties too. This was such a contrast to Rainbow Training but I relished the challenge. This worked well, too, with mentoring prospective Commissioners. It was so good to see them develop their management and leadership skills and I found great satisfaction in the realisation that perhaps I'd had a small hand in their progress.

I became a Trainer Tutor, which I also enjoyed, though the vast distances to travel across the Region, for evening meetings with my prospective trainers, proved to be rather difficult, after my full-time work at College. Session observation on a Saturday were not such a problem.

A surprise reunion

It was whilst attending a Training Day in Greater London, to observe one of my 'prospectives', that I came across one of my old Guides from 7th Plumstead Common Company. We were reunited during a lull in the proceedings.

I had decided to give my prospective some 'space' to train without me breathing down her neck. So I grabbed a coffee and began chatting to the County Training Chairman. I enquired where she was from and Plumsted Common was mentioned.

We quickly realised that we had known each other over 30 years before and that she had actually been one of my Guides. Anne had been in the Guard of Honour outside All Saint's Church, Shooters Hill, on the occasion of my first marriage. She can be seen on the step below and in front of me, in the photograph.

I was so pleased to hear that Guiding formed a huge part of her life too, and that her disability hadn't impeded her success.

Almost my last appointment

How the years have flown by since that very quiet and shy Brownie first made her Promise all those years ago, in 1949. I have 'Guided' in eight different Counties and four Regions. I have held numerous appointments and made so many like-minded friends. What fantastic experiences too. Guiding is my life, and my life – well, a goodly portion, is Guiding.

The magic '65' approached really fast (in the days when the age of 65 indicated retirement from active involvement with the girls). I was able to keep my Training Appointment until then. I had become an Associate Member of the Trefoil Guild in Selsey though, at that time sadly, my heart was not really with them. Somehow, I just couldn't get my head around the fact that becoming a Trefoil member would be good.

What was I to do? I didn't feel that I was actively Guiding anymore and I felt as if there was a huge hole in my life.

Angela to the rescue

It was at this time, when I felt I had no Guiding purpose, that I received a letter from our County Commissioner, Angela, asking me to become a County Vice President. I was needed again – wonderful. Thank you so much Angela.

Goodbye to Selsey

Towards the end of 2008, Ron and I decided to move to Hayling Island to be nearer Karyn and family and my next phase of Guiding began.

**'I'm sharing my passion for Guiding with others,
and steering them forward, whatever their need'**

Chapter Nine

'And now I am President of Sussex West County.
An honour and privilege – yet humbling task'

Vice President

I took up my appointment as a County Vice President in May, 2007 and it was immensely rewarding. I loved being invited to District, Division and County events and meet with the girls and their leaders. It was good to see 'Guiding in Action' and know that Guiding in Sussex West was still going from strength to strength.

I was fortunate to be invited to most Division Centenary Celebrations and had the time of my life sharing activities with the girls. I tried diabling, walking on stilts, riding on a merry-go-round (several times), abseiling and more. Guiding is such fun, whatever age you are.

It was good to be invited to non-Guiding functions too, as it enabled me to enthuse about our 'great Guiding game' and spread the word about our wonderful organisation.

Whilst a Vice President I managed, once again, to acquire tickets for the Thinking Day Service at Westminster Abbey. I had sufficient for Karyn, Abiee and Louisa too.

Abiee was ready to make her Promise as a Guide and, with permission from her Guide Leader and Commissioner, she made it on the chancel steps of the Abbey after the service. This was a very special moment for me, marred only by the fact that I lost 'the badge' and had to borrow one!!!! I have never been allowed to forget that. Who knows, maybe in years to come, Abiee's badge will surface somewhere in the Abbey.

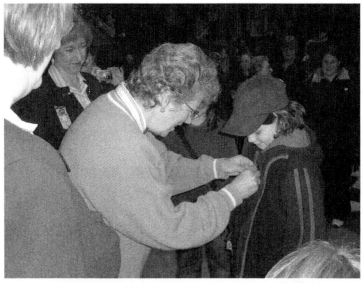

On the chancel steps: I am with Angela, CC Sussex West and LaSER's Region Commissioner. Abiee is with Louisa, Kez and Laura

In 2011, Angela's successor, Annabel, invited me to become President of the County. This was such a tremendous honour and I relished all opportunities to support Annabel and Sussex West members in this wonderful movement, whilst continuing to 'shout to the world' just how fantastic Guiding is. I felt that the Vice Presidents needed more of an active role and so here was my chance, as President, to encourage more pro-action.

Fund Raising – God's Golden Acre

I began with a fund-raising campaign. LaSER Region was involved in a project in Africa entitled 'God's Golden Acre'.

The story of God's Golden Acre began when a South African woman, Heather Reynolds, came across a remote village in a neighbouring country. A baby's cry was heard from one of the huts. Inquiring of her local companion, she found out that the child was one of a dozen or so left behind to look after themselves as their parents had died of AIDS.

Back in South Africa, Heather researched the AIDS pandemic situation & quickly discovered the situation would develop in the same way there. Very soon, the Reynolds family opened up their home to the very sick & dying children in their area. They soon had 41 children in their home, and this was the beginning of 'God's Golden Acre'. There are now some 92 children living with the Reynolds, with a proportional number of care-givers & volunteers.

God's Golden Acre - Today

God's Golden Acre, Khayelihle, is a non profit making charity involved in the care of children who have been orphaned or abandoned because of HIV/AIDS related illness & violence.

Rather than simply putting the children in orphanages, God's Golden Acre, Khayelihle, primarily strives to keep children in their community setting by assisting families using various initiatives to support themselves.

Their aim is to achieve the following:

To provide children with a good education

To assist them to become well-adjusted adults

To develop the natural talents & aptitudes of each & every child

To provide a caring, loving, nurturing & compassionate community environment

Several of the senior members and young adults in Sussex West had been to Africa to carry out service in the form of building schools and working with the children, and so much fund raising was on going. I challenged our VPs and, with their almost unanimous support, we were able to contribute a substantial amount to this cause.

Lodge Hill

Another project was at Lodge Hill, an inclusive outdoor activity centre with residential facilities, situated within 32 acres of stunning woodland in the midst of the South Downs National Park, overlooking the Arun Valley near Pulborough.

I had organised a lunch here as a social get together for us and, during our tour of the grounds after lunch, we were shown the Karting Race Track. Around the edge of the track were large advertising boards, such as found around any race track. There were local business boards, and one advertisng the Scouts – but no Guides!! It was a no brainer – we needed to 'be there'. The VPs were 100% behind me and within a few months, our Guide board was in situ.

Annual Review in Arundel Castle

'From the 11th century, the castle has served as a home and has been in the ownership of the family of the Duke of Norfolk for over 400 years. It is the principal seat of the Howard family, whose heads have been first Earls of Arundel and then Dukes of Norfolk. It is a Grade I listed building.'

I suppose the major event for me each year was chairing the Annual Review in the Baron's Hall at Arundel Castle. I'd already had a practice as I took the chair as a VP when my predecessor was unable to be there. This was always a very resplendent and sumptuous affair and I loved carrying out my role.

The Reviews were always very well attended and we had tremendous support from the Mayors, Councillors, other youth organisations, including the Scouts and Sea Rangers, and of course, the leaders themselves. We always hoped to see Georgina, Duchess of Norfolk and our Patron, who kindly allowed us to meet in her Castle every year. She was always, and still is, incredibly busy, so it was a bonus when she was able to join us.

Margaret and I receiving our 40 years' Service Certificates and badges from Region Chief Commissioner, Pip Mc Kerrow , during the Annual Review in 2015

I was invited, a few times, to have coffee with Georgina in the Castle. I was always intrigued by the loo in her private quarters as it was just as you might imagine in a castle – in a little turreted room, but the modern loo seemed rather out of place. Her kitchen was 'totally normal' with a range and rather old-fashioned kitchen cupboards. This was some years ago now, so things could have changed. I did smile when my coffee was brought to me, by the butler, and placed on a small round table next to my chair – the type of round table, years ago, that would have had a round tablecloth draped over it that reached to the floor. There was never a tablecloth – just bare MDF!!

Now lunch was a totally different matter. On several occasions we VPs were invited to lunch – and this was always just as you would expect from a Duchess – absolutely perfect in everyway. We were always fearful of breaking the very high quality bone-china and crystal glassware, and making sure that we used the correct cutlery.

President's Challenge

'What can the Vice Presidents do for the girls in Sussex West to help them celebrate Girlguiding's Centenary?'

That was the question put to me, when I became President, by Dena, past County President. So, my mind began working and the seed was sown for 'The Challenge'.

My vision was for every girl in the County, from Rainbows through to Guides, to take part in something that would give them an insight into Guiding in earlier times, but link with and show relevance to today's programme. Initially, my plan was for Senior Section to help in the organisation but it was suggested that they might like to take part too.

I also wanted every girl to achieve something tangible so some of the activities were linked to the Heritage/History of Guiding Badges, thus enabling the participants to gain Interest Badges on their journey.

Of course, my original challenge was far too lengthy and, over the course of time, a dedicated team from County adjusted the activities – and so the President's Challenge finally came to fruition in 2013.

It was so good to hear of the preparations and planning in units, ready for the Division finals which took place early in June. I was able to visit Lodge Hill for Petworth Division's weekend of activities. It was a joy to see the girls taking part so enthusiastically - great excitement at times and more serious moments when it mattered. I was impressed with their knowledge of first aid and smiled to myself at the 'not so edible' pancakes cooked by the Guides on buddy burners. I hasten to add that not all the pancakes were inedible. Of course, the singing was very dear to my heart too.

Billingshurst Guides
practising their action song

Another term and with the summer break behind us, it was soon time for the County Final on 21st September at Brinsbury College. Sadly, not all finalists were able to come on the day but all those there really entered into the spirit of the occasion and very ably proved their knowledge after their months of preparation.

What amazing structures were made by the Rainbows from 'recyclables' – a magnificent tower for Rapunzel, complete with long, flowing fair hair and an equally resplendent castle. The concentration on faces was a picture when '20 skips backwards' were attempted. Feely bags were prodded, pictures and banners scrutinised and approved, leaves & fruits were recognised and our youngest members so ably proved their worth with all their activities.

Just watching the girls brought back so many memories for me. The Brownies throwing their beanbag overarm reminded me of when I had to do that for my Brownie First Class Badge. My ball went sailing over the wall – never to be found again!! How neatly the Brownies folded their clothes too. I just wonder if they always do that at home now. I suspect not!!

Sewing on a button – what a useful skill and most made a good attempt at that. Message carrying, composition of the Union Flag, knowing what to do if clothing catches fire, posters and banners – so many memories for 'us oldies' and all these included in the Brownies' Challenge.

The Guides ably demonstrated their 'pitching & striking a ridge tent' skills, and in rolling along the folded canvas to flatten it to a suitable size to be packed away. I'd forgotten just how long camp gadgets take to make but it was so good to see the teams working together and supporting each other in this task – the finished products being much more sophisticated than ours ever were!!

Teams had to show proficiency in reading a map, using a compass, message carrying and Scout's Pace, singing camp fire songs and two verses of the National Anthem, as well as proving knowledge of some aspect of Guiding history. The teams were kept very busy.

After a hectic day, the afternoon finished with a yummy cake (made by Amanda – (I was so impressed) and a drink, whilst marks were added and collated. Badges were presented to all participants, including leaders, judges and helpers and finally it was 'results time' when certificates and prizes were presented.

Sadly, there could be just one winner in each section but all teams were to be congratulated on their achievements. The results were close but clear winners at the end.

I was so grateful to Annabel and County team members for their support and considerable organisation, to Trefoil Guild members, families and friends for their help along the way, to the judges and Vice Presidents for giving up their precious time, to the leaders for encouraging their unit members and most of all – to the girls for taking part.

So, the vision I had in 2009 became a reality and I was delighted with the outcome. So much work by so many people provided the 'we discover, we grow' experience for the girls, just as I had hoped for.

Here I am leading 'One finger, one thumb keep moving,' at a Brownie Day at Paulton's Park

Another change

I so enjoyed my President's role but the mileage I was doing was considerable as I was living in Hampshire and making frequent visits to Sussex. This was not only putting mileage on 'the clock' but costing a considerable amount too. With Trefoil membership money and Girlguiding's, I felt I needed to pull in the reins and so, with regret, gave up the position of President.

I missed it dreadfully, and still do – and maybe my decision was too hastily made. The clock cannot be turned back though and I really enjoy my Trefoil activities. I have kept my Girlguiding membership but pay directly to CHQ, thus saving a fair few pounds each year. 'Every little helps' as 'Mr. Tesco' says!! My role terminated at the end of January, 2015.

So, 2015 saw me concentrating solely on Trefoil activities.

'**Supporting our members, promoting and sharing**
My passion for Guiding – what more could I ask'.

Chapter Ten

'Today I'm in Trefoil, loving each moment,
Supporting, promoting our great Guiding game'

Hayling to the rescue

We moved to Hayling at the end of October, 2008, and after a wonderful holiday in the Caribbean to celebrate Ron's 80th birthday, and a fantastic Christmas with Karyn and family, 2009 was soon upon us. I attended my first meeting of Hayling Island Trefoil Guild in January 2009.

This was the first time, for many, many years, that I had attended a Guiding function where I hadn't known anyone. But, within Guiding, there are instant friends and I felt part of the 'Hayling family' straight away. I joined with a very positive attitude and with determination too, that becoming a full member of Trefoil was going to be right for me – and it is. I'm just loving it.

Dark Horse

I had heard about the Dark Horse Venture from my Sussex West friends and Liz, a one time fellow District Commissioner, had been the County Coordinator for the scheme in Sussex West. I decided I wanted to find out more and take up the challenge but none of our Hayling members had heard about it, and were not able to help.

So, how could I go about it?

I decided to contact Marian, Secretary of Hampshire East Trefoil. We had met in the past whilst she was County Commissioner and I a Trainer. It was a starting point. Marian put me in touch with Elizabeth and Margaret, who had been joint coordinators in the past, and I duly visited them.

More than I bargained for

What a pleasant afternoon we had. Of course, no one in Trefoil ever has trouble in chatting do they? The time just flew by. I learned about the scheme and heard of Elizabeth's and Margaret's experiences, but what I hadn't bargained for was that I would leave their house with a folder and directory – having somehow agreed to take on the role of coordinator in the County, subject to our Chairman's approval, of course.

And so it was, in June 2009, I began my own Dark Horse adventures and, whilst doing so, hoped to enthuse other members in the County too.

My first County Meeting

I was invited to the County meeting in September, to explain about the scheme. I couldn't believe how many faces were there from the past – from trainers, Commissioners, Guiders I had trained, and even a fellow passenger who had travelled to Switzerland with her husband and Guides. We had shared a coach from London to Interlaken. It was so good to meet up with everyone again.

Powerpoint

I had never put a Powerpoint presentation together but decided that I needed the challenge and that Powerpoint would certainly help me in the delivery of my presentation to 'sell' the Venture to Guilds. I actually thoroughly enjoyed compiling it and playing with the fonts, colours and images. But would it be suitable?

My Guild helped me out and agreed to become the 'guinea pigs'. Having given their approval, I gave my first proper presentation to Portsmouth South Guild in the November.

Support from home

I was very anxious not to neglect Ron, whilst touring the County 'touting' for new Dark Horse participants. He seemed to enjoy being my chauffeur and taking charge of the screen. It was good to have him involved; he was company on the journeys and, being a Hampshire hog', knew Hampshire far better than I.

Venturing on

I so enjoyed travelling around the county, visiting Guilds, meeting their members and giving the necessary help and support. It was very worthwhile with about 20 members from around the County participating at any one time.

Receiving my Gold Dark Horse Venture Award
from Rose, Trefoil County Chairman

The Centenary 2009/2010

How wonderful it was to be able to join in the launch celebrations in September, 2009, not only with Hayling Island Trefoil but with Karyn, Abiee and Louisa too, knowing that we were all in the same Division.

We enjoyed an incredibly busy year with several 'Mountain Top Moments'.

Westminster Abbey

Way back in February, 2009, Hilary Chittock, whom Karyn and I have known for many years, explained that she would be 'Lead Volunteer' for the special Centenary Thinking Day Service in Westminster Abbey in February, 2010. She had an idea to involve a family of several generations and might we be interested. Of course we were.

So, in October of that year, we began to compile the 'conversation' for 'Reflections', endeavouring to show how the Promise and values of the Movement have influenced and shaped the lives of successive generations of girls and women.

What fun we had putting this together, far too long initially. It bounced back and forth for several months between us, Hilary, the Dean and CHQ. The final script was approved and our big moment drew closer.

Frantic practices were held locally, centenary shirts and neckers prepared and finally the day arrived. What an occasion and what a tremendous experience. It was one never to be forgotten and certainly a 'Mountain Top Moment' for us all.

Here we are, in Westminster Abbey, standing by the Memorial to Lord Baden-Powell, and Olave, his wife and World Chief Guide.

Guiding Magazine

For the Centenary, it had been decided to produce Guiding (Magazine) quarterly in a new format. Somehow, our involvement in the Westminster Abbey Service had initiated interest in our family story and we found ourselves being interviewed for the new magazine. The article (see below) appeared on the day of the service – another 'Mountain Top Moment – and Abiee and Louisa were delighted when Liz Burnley, Chief Guide, asked them to sign her copy.

Keep it in the family   *A story of four generations united by guiding*

*(article from Guiding Magazine Spring 2010
- used by kind permission of Jane Yettram, Editor)*

Guiding was a bit different from how it is today when Hilda Warburton joined in 1916. She camped in a bell tent, stuffed a bag with straw for a mattress and gained badges such as Sick Nurse, Laundress and Thrift.

'I wished I'd talked much more to Mum about her guiding while she was alive', says

Hilda's daughter, Avril Stouse. 'I would love to know how the meetings were organised, about her guiding friends, Patrol names. The list goes on. Sadly, all the time I was a Brownie, Guide, Ranger and Leader, I was so involved that I didn't give much thought to what had happened in the past. But it was that past that shaped my guiding experiences and I'm so thankful for that.'

It's those little details of guiding's past, as well as memories of the big events, that the Centenary Story Bank, one of guiding's Heritage Projects, wants to preserve. The aim is to capture the experiences of members, both from long ago and more recent times, to create a lasting record of the impact guiding has had on individuals and society throughout its first 100 years.

With four generations involved, the guiding history of Avril's family spans much of the last century. She is now County Vice-President of Sussex West and a Trefoil Guild member with Hayling Island Guild in Hampshire. Her daughter, Karyn Harris, was a Brownie, Guide, Young Leader, and later leader and trainer. Karyn's daughters Abiee, 13, and Louisa, 10 are members of 1st West Hayling Guides, Hampshire.

Avril first made her Promise as a Brownie in 1949 and she treasures memories of those early days. 'It rained at my first camp but I don't remember it dampening our spirit', she recalls.

'Sweets had only recently come off rationing and I spent my whole allowance of pocket money on Mars bars which I placed under my pillow to keep them safe. The next morning my long hair was tangled in a sticky, chocolatey, gooey mess'!

But as a Guide, Avril made huge efforts to keep up appearances. 'I always had a pressed blouse and skirt with pristine tie three fingers from my polished belt, shiny shoes and the requisite pencil, paper, string, fourpence for a phone call, and a brushed beret with badge over my left eye. We were allowed to remove berets for games! Mum instilled in me that my Promise Badge must always be polished on the back as well as the front. Even though it couldn't be seen, it showed that you were a true Guide and doing your best at all times, even when others couldn't see'.

Karyn agrees. 'I watch my girls go off to Guides in their jeans and trainers and think, Gosh! I never would have got away with that. But the guiding ethos hasn't changed at all. They may not polish their shoes but the pride is still there'.

All the fundraising and community projects undertaken by members today also show that the commitment to helping others has continued from those early days. 'I remember Mum often talking about the poor children in Woolwich, London, where she was a Guide and how they'd mend clothes and collect shoes for them'. says Avril.

Like many younger members, Abiee and Louisa love to hear guiding stories from the past. 'Mum told me about when she was a Brownie and she gave a little cross-stitched mat to the Queen and when, on a Young Leaders' weekend, she and her friends climbed onto the balcony where the adults were and hung spiders over their heads! I never realised she was so naughty!' says Abiee.

So what does their long involvement in guiding mean to them as a family?

'I used to feel really proud carrying the flag when I was young,' says Karyn. Then Abiee was asked to carry the flag in the local parade. It's something else watching your children do what you have done, what your mum has done and your grandma has done before that.'

'We believe in the same guiding ideals and we've shared so much fun', adds Avril. 'Now that Abiee and Louisa are keen members too, it's just so good to be able to share a common interest, each at our own level.'

Having missed the chance to explore the history and ideals of guiding more through her mum, Avril is writing her own guiding history to pass on to Karyn, Abiee and Louisa. Luckily, Karyn has always been a keen scrapbooker and so has a record of her mountain-top moments. such as when she was in Switzerland in 1992 to celebrate the 60th birthday of Our Chalet.

'I actually wrote in my scrapbook that singing the World Song would never be the same again and it hasn't. It will always conjure up memories of standing on that beautiful mountain singing with Guides from all over the world.'

Abiee and Louisa are already planning how they're going to record their own special experiences during the Centenary year.

'I plan to make a memory box using one of the Centenary biscuit tins (once I have eaten all the biscuits myself, of course!)'. says Abiee. 'I want to keep photos and mementos. I can begin by putting in the photo of my sister and me with Mum and Nanna at the Centenary Party.'

'I'm going to make a scrapbook of all my activities and make sure that I record what happened,' says Louisa. I know that Nanna is disappointed that she doesn't know much about her mum's guiding history and so I want to make a record of mine'.

Centenary of Girlguiding

More Mountain Top Moments

During the course of the year, I was asked if I would be willing to give the talk at Petworth Division's special Centenary Thinking Day Service in Petworth Church. Actually, I was asked if I would say a 'few words', which usually means thanking everyone for coming etc, but, as the conversation progressed, I realised that these 'few words' were obviously meant to be more than that. Taking this special part in the service was a magic moment for me as it was in Petworth Division that I spent my early days, when first arriving in Sussex. What a sea of faces were before me as I stood in the pulpit with my flannel and bowl of water. To find out more about this, you will have to read the appendix.

The City of London Guildhall

These wonderful occasions and experiences continued throughout 2010.

Just after the Thinking Day Service, I received an invitation, from the City of London Corporation, inviting me to the Guildhall to attend an Early Evening Reception to mark the Centenary of Girlguiding UK on Wednesday 21st April, 2010. I had no idea how this invitation was initiated but, of course, I accepted. I could find no one I knew who had also received an invitation but, undeterred, I set off for London and enjoyed a truly magnificent day.

I booked myself into ICANDO at CHQ for the morning and ambled around the Centenary Exhibition. My lunch was eaten in the members' room downstairs and then, in the afternoon, it was off to the Apollo Theatre in Victoria to see the musical, Wicked, and it was 'wicked' to use the vernacular of my granddaughters at the time. Sadly, I had to leave before the end in order to arrive at the Guildhall in time.

Now, what a tremendous occasion this was. The champagne flowed and canapes were in abundance. We walked through a guard of honour made up of local Brownies, with mostly brown faces and wide eyes, with huge, infectious smiles. They were so bubbly and excited – truly portraying the ethos of Guiding. What a welcome.

Now, I did say that I knew no one, locally, that was going, but of course, when I entered the room, I immediately spotted so many faces I knew. What a reunion of like-minded people. I couldn't believe how quickly the time disappeared. The reception was meant to finish at 7.30 and when I eventually looked at my watch it was already nearing 8.00pm and still so many people I hadn't managed to catch up with.

I was fortunate in being able to chat to Liz Burnley, Chief Guide, and also Margaret

Routledge, National Trefoil Chairman, as well as meeting new friends and old. It was truly inspiring.

Could my Guiding experiences get any better? Of course they could. Guiding continues to offer such experiences, whether you are actively Guiding or in Trefoil.

Wall to wall enjoyment

What a fantastic time I had during those wonderful Centenary Celebrations. Fun, fellowship and friendship shone out the whole time and so many new experiences too.

I would never have imagined having the time of my life riding on a merry-go-round at Sussex West's Party in the Park at Fontwell Racecourse.

Nor would I have envisaged that I would abseil down the tower at Foxlease, as one who doesn't like heights and goes all 'swimmy headed' when up high with no enclosure around. Strange that I can ride cable cars, gondolas, the London Eye, Singapore Flyer, Burj Kalifa. Climb lighthouses and church towers, go up the Eiffel and Tokyo Towers-just as long as they are covered in with a strong barrier to hold on to.

HELP – I'm not sure I like this!

Are we nearly there yet?

'Actually, I really enjoyed that'. Would I do it again? Not sure!

It's fortunate that the Spinnaker Tower, in Portsmouth falls into the 'enclosed category' for the Centenary Celebrations took me to the top on two occasions. Firstly, was the invitation to join Hampshire East's special day there to coincide with the Girlguiding sponsored Tall Ship's mooring at Gun Wharf. Neighbouring Counties were invited too, hence my meeting up with Sheila.

Secondly, we enjoyed a Bucks Fizz reception with Hampshire East's Girlguiding and Trefoil members. Both occasions were so memorable and enjoyable.

Sheila and I standing on the glass floor in the Spinnaker Tower

Open House at Foxlease

Foxlease held an 'Open House' Day just before the official ending of the Centenary celebrations. It was wonderful to be taken back in time as we walked through the rooms.

What a surprise awaited us in 'South Africa', for there was 'Lady BP' taking a break from her journal and ready to welcome us. Actually, when alone with 'her' it was good to chat with Charlotte in the morning and later Barbara – both of whom took on the role with great aplomb.

Of course, I must mention my friends Margaret and Sue, the serving maids, who greeted guests in the entrance hall and occupied themselves in the making of pomanders.

Such a good day and what an opportunity to show off our lovely Princess Mary House to the public.

'100 years of Memories'

Foxlease was the venue for Hampshire East's Trefoil '100 years of Memories', where members dressed in costumes depicting the last 100 years and undertook a range of activities – some more challenging than others, but all enjoyable. The day finished with a Barn Dance followed by a Campfire Sing. We crawled home after an exhausting but fantastic day.

International Centenary Camp

It was wonderful to be able to help for a day at the International
Camp at Lyons Copse and meet up with Abiee and Louisa, who were having the time of their lives. I derived so much pleasure in seeing them actively involved and obviously enjoying their Guiding. My Mum would have been immensely proud.

29th October 2010 – aka 20.10, 20.10. 20.10

This was an amazing day that began in Portsmouth, in the morning, for Hampshire East's Trefoil Fellowship Service where timings were 'jiggled' and we renewed our Promise at 'twenty past ten'. What a wealth of Guiding experience was in St. Mark's Church at that time.

We then returned to our own Divisions to take part in the finale of the Centenary. From the youngest Rainbows to the oldest Trefoil members, we were all there, with past members too.

Karyn, Abiee, Louisa and I thoroughly enjoyed celebrating together
with Hayling Island Division.

We gathered in the Radford Guide Hall in the evening, and enjoyed hot dogs and fizzy pop or hot chocolate and a very raucous campfire, before gathering on the field to renew Promises.

How our young people enjoyed their evening, and so did 'us oldies'- particularly when we gathered around the blazing campfire when everyone else had disappeared to the field. We sang nostalgically some of our old favourite songs – ones the girls of today no longer sing, sadly.

It was truly memorable, especially when we joined Guiding sisters throughout the country to reaffirm our Promise on **20.10 at 20.10 in 20.10**.

Sea Rangers celebrate 90 years

Though there are no longer Sea Rangers within Girlguiding, the Sea Rangers Association is still in existence. 2010 also saw the 90th birthday celebrations of the Sea Rangers and a special anniversary service was held at St. Ann's Church, Portsmouth Dockyard. I was fortunate to receive an invitation through my connection with the Chairman, a regular guest at Sussex West's Annual Meetings.

Chris and Helen, standing with me at the end of the service, are members of Portsmouth South Trefoil but have also kept up their membership of the Sea Ranger Association.

End of an era and on to the next

So now we are on our way towards the next hundred years of Girlguiding. One thing I know for sure is that I won't be around for the Bi-Centenary celebrations, though I hope some of my descendants will be taking a full part in them. But I shall never know.

Trefoil goes Cruising

Whenever Ron and I go cruising, I try to arrange a meet up of Trefoil members who may be on board. This has been very successful and I've met members from the UK and beyond.

This is the 'Oriana' Trefoil, meeting up on board for a Thinking Day ceremony in 2008.

We were in Hong Kong on Thinking Day, 2011 and I managed to make contact with Hong Kong Guide Headquarters. Ron and I were invited for the day to join the staff in their Thinking Day Ceremony. This was carried out in Cantonese but Serena, the Chief Executive and our host, translated as it progressed. We hardly needed the translation as we could follow proceedings very easily – the same Guiding ceremonies happen throughout the world, it would seem.

Trefoil members are 'Golden Girls' in Hong Kong! I really do prefer our name. 'Golden Girls' aside, it was a very special day.

Thinking day, Hong Kong
22nd February 2011 • Hong Kong Girl Guide Headquarters

Voyage Award

It was early in 2013 that Val, our County Chairman, asked me to represent her at the Trefoil Conference, to be held at Swanwick near Derby, as she was unable to go. There was to be a new Trefoil Challenge, entitled the Voyage Award, akin to the Dark Horse Venture but specifically for Trefoil members. It was to be launched this weekend.

It was a good conference and I met up with friends from around the Country, including Margaret from Sussex and Sheila from Cornwall. I liked the new award, signed up to begin the challenge (the 5th in the country to do so) and planned how I was going to introduce it to members in our County.

For a time, both awards ran side by side and some members were working towards both. Eventually, due to the fact that the Government withdrew its grant from the Dark Horse Venture and the success of the Voyage Award, the DHV ceased. My new role in the County therefore became 'Voyage Coordinator'. It was good to visit members around the county and help and support them whilst I was undertaking my own challenges.

A special invitation

I had always enjoyed going to the Thinking Day Service in Westminster Abbey each year and was very saddened to hear that the Centenary Service in February, 2010, was to be the last. However, imagine my delight when I received an invitation to attend a 'National Scout and Guide Service of Celebration and Thanksgiving' for November 2013. Huge disappointment followed when I realised that Ron and I would be on a cruise. Thankfully, the invitation was reissued and Karyn, as my guest, and I travelled to London the following year. We enjoyed the service, felt priviledged to have been invited and it was so good for both Karyn and I to meet up with so many friends in the Abbey.

Karyn and I outside Westminster Abbey
after the service

'Sing Together'

For one of my Voyage challenges, I compiled a County Trefoil Song Book. My idea grew from the fact that, whenever I led the singing at Trefoil functions, too many books were needed and members just didn't have them all in their possession. It was becoming costly to print out words of the songs I wished to introduce each time.

So, 'Sing Together' was compiled and available to purchase from Amazon. Profits were ploughed straight back into County funds, so, at a cost of £5.00, the books sold well, which helped both members and County funds.

Leading a 'Brownie sing' at Sandy Acres

'Long Legged Sailor' at Lyons Copse

County Annual Report

The Voyage Award was in its second year when I began to compile the Annual County Report. I was able to use this as one of my activities for the Silver Level. Having previously 'put together' the Song Book, I was now more conversant with the organisation of material and its setting up, ready for print. The hardest part was, and still is, persuading the contributors to send in their reports in time! It's very satisfying to hold in your hand, something you have helped to produce. I'm now, as I write, collecting individual reports for the 2020 edition.

Trefoil celebrates 75 years

What a busy year it was in 2018. Trefoil had reached 75 years (a year younger than me) and there were celebrations, celebrations, celebrations. It was such a fun filled year which began on Thinking Day with a sunrise ceremony on the top of Portsdown Hill and a sausage bap breakfast after.

Eunice and I had written a book about the history of Trefoil in Hampshire, Trefoil 75, since its beginning and Thinking Day was its launch. We enjoyed putting it together and had learnt much whilst undertaking our research. It seemed a fitting way to mark the 75th birthday.

TREFOIL 75

compiled by Avril Stouse & Eunice Conybeare

Hampshire East Celebrates
75 years of Trefoil Guild

'Trefoil Guild is Guiding for Adults. This book has been written to commemorate 75 years of Trefoil Guild from its early beginnings in the County of Hampshire and, from 1970, Hampshire East County. Memories, stories and information have been gathered together from personal recollections, log books, archives and County Reports and each Guild in Hampshire East has contributed in some way.'

As a result of writing the book, I was asked to be the guest speaker at Hampshire West's Trefoil Annual Meeting, in March of that year, to talk about the History of

Trefoil Guild in Hampshire. My Powerpoint presentations had developed over the years and I was able to incorporate video clips and Guiding songs from the past. What fun we all had in joining in those songs known only by Trefoil members. It was a trip down memory lane and most enjoyable for me, and my audience, too, I do believe.

In April, Trefoil members from London and South East Region were having a celebratory weekend at Lakeside, one of the Warners' Holiday Viilages on Haylimg. I was delighted to receive an invitation to join them for lunch and their special afternoon How lovely it was to catch up with so many Trefoil friends from my old Region.

Also, in April, we had our own county celebration, at Stansted House. Lots of activities on offer throughout the day and the house was opened up especially for us. It was a scorching hot day, and we had concerns about inclement weather!!! True to form, being a Trefoil gathering, we enjoyed a delicious cream tea at the end of the day.

Receiving a Trefoil 'Thanks Badge' and certificate
from Margaret, County Trefoil Chair

Our South West Region Annual Meeting was held in Weymouth in May – another fun weekend with a special celebratory meal on the Saturday evening. My good friend Margaret, from Sussex, was celebrating her own 75th birthday that weekend and we had been invited to her party, in Sussex, on the Sunday. I sent her a message from Weymouth on the Sunday morning to wish her 'Many Happy Returns' and we then 'hotfooted it' to Worthing. How surprised Margaret was when we arrived. 'I thought you were in Weymouth', she said. It was lovely to celebrate Margaret's special birthday as well as Trefoil's.

We journeyed to Birmingham for the National Annual Meeting – another very special celebratory one. The Saturday evening saw the audience dressed in Abba style and bopping in the aisles. We may be more 'mature' in years but certainly not in mind!!!

No sooner had we arrived home than we were off, to Foxlease this time, for the Three Hampshire Counties Trefoil Day. Lots on offer again and I had my chance to 'zip-wire'.

Weeeeeeeeeeeee. It was great.

At the end of the day, Foxlease treated us all to a – you've guessed it – a delicious cream tea.

The three 'Hampshires' joined together again in September for a wonderful Commemorative Service in Romsey Abbey. Once more, I had a task – to present a short snippet on 'Hampshire Trefoil History'. Our book contained 206 pages and I was restricted to one side of A4 – not easy – but I managed. It was truly amazing, standing at the lectern, and seeing Trefoil friends aplenty. Such a moving and memorable service and the Girlguiding World Flag flew resplendently from the Abbey Tower. There was no mistaking that 'the Guides were back in town'.

Girlguidng Hampshire East invited all Trefoil members in the County to a cream tea at the Marriott Hotel. More sumptuous food and such a good opportunity to meet and mingle with our Girlguiding friends., It was a splendid afternoon.

Train Trek

What a finish we had to our year of celebrations. We enjoyed a fabulous 'Train Trek'. All counties in the Region had a 'Meet Up Steam Up' in their own county or a neighbouring one, and members joined in locally, with some going to all venues. You have probably guessed that Ron and I 'did' them all!

We began in Jersey and finished in Windsor, riding on Heritage railways and meeting the public. Sadly, so few know about Trefoil so it was a wonderful idea of our Region PR Adviser, Frances, to 'spread the word' about us.

Date	Destination	Itinerary	Accommodation
Tuesday 2nd October	Travel to Jersey	Travel to Jersey by Ferry from tbc	Jersey
Wednesday 3rd October	Jersey		Jersey
Thursday 4th October	Jersey	Pallet Steam Train Museum	Jersey
Friday 5th October	Travel to Guernsey	Sausmarez Manor	Guernsey

Saturday 6th October	Guernsey		Guernsey
Sunday 7th October	Guernsey		Guernsey
Monday 8th October	Travel to Toddington		Toddington
Tuesday 9th October	Toddington Station GL54 5DT	MU-SU, train ride. Travel to Bodmin area	Bodmin
Wednesday 10th October	Bodmin & Wenford Steam Railway	MU-SU	Bodmin
Thursday 11th October	Keynsham Guide HQ Ashton Way	Travel from Bodmin to Keynsham	Keynsham
Friday 12th October	Coach leaves Guide HQ 8.00am	MU-SU STEAM Philly Castle Hall 10.30am Travel to Bitton Station for MU-SU 2.00pm	Keynsham
Saturday 13th October	Coach collects from Premier Inn 7.00am	Bishop's Lydeard 10.20 train to Minehead MU-SU 12.00 Coach departs 12.30 for Buckfastleigh or Totnes TBC. MU-SU Coach departs for Swanage at 5.00pm. Fish & chips at West Bay. Arrive Swanage 8.30pm	Swanage
Sunday 14th October	10.00 train to Harman's Cross MU-SU 10.15. WW2 event at Community Centre. Coach loaded at 11.30 to depart at 11.45 for Alresford	MU-SU Alresford Depart on train for Alton. Coach to Slough. Train for Windsor GWR train. 3.30 MU-SU 3.30pm. Cream Tea Harte & Garter. Return to coach & back to Keynsham.	Keynsham
Monday 15th October	Home		

At each venue, the specially made banner was paraded and handed over to the next County. Our 'Meet Up, Steam Up,' for Hampshire was at Alton at the Watercress Line.

The 'Train Trek Banner' being presented in Jersey

Ron, Eunice and I meeting up with Cornish friends on Bodmin Station

The two weeks culminated in a final ceremony at Windsor where the banner was finally presented by the replica 'Queen' Steam Engine at Windsor Station, before we adjourned to the 'Harte and Garter' for the final cream tea. It had been an amazing end to our year of celebrations.

'If you can't beat 'em, join 'em'

As time went on and Ron got to know more and more Trefoil friends, he decided to become a member too. I suppose, by this time, he had 'endured' 20 years of supporting me in my Guiding activities and was getting used to the idea that I was 'very involved'. It's good to have him as a fellow member and, since then, another husband has joined Hayling Trefoil.

New County Role

At the end of our 75th Celebratory year, I was asked if I would consider taking on the Public Relations Adviser role. This was something I had never even contemplated, always leaving PR to those 'who knew'. However, I had been the Dark Horse Venture and Voyage Award Coordinator since arriving in Hampshire ten years before, so maybe it was time for a change and I was certainly ready for another challenge. My new appointment, therefore, began at the beginning of 2019.

As well as continuing to compile the Annual Report, I decided to produce 'e-news' as a tool to keep our members, Girlguiding members, dignitaries, MPs, councillors, the local community and friends in touch with what is happening in Hampshire East Trefoil throughout the year. This was a huge learning curve for me as I tried to come to terms with the intricacies of 'Mailchimp'. I managed, and three mailings were sent out in 2019, and these have been well received, so worth the effort.

With emphasis on recruitment, parents of Girlguiding members were targeted. I'm not aware that any have joined but at least Trefoil was brought to their attention.

To help the public become more aware of Trefoil, I devised a 'County Strapline',

'Let's be seen in 2019'.

And we have been. Our display boards, literature and banner have been taken 'on the road' whenever there was an opportunity to do so. Trefoil members have been encouraged to wear Trefoil scarves, polo shirts and badges and to talk about Trefoil whenever possible.

We need to **'Be seen a-plenty in 2020'**

I cannot begin to put into words how much I have gained from being a member of our wonderful organization. Guiding has given me a truly wonderful and inspiring 70 years.

Thank you, **B-P,** for your far-reaching vision all those years ago.

**'I've noticed the changes since I've been a member but
The Spirit of Guiding remains just the same'.**

My Guiding Heritage

I wonder if I would have been such a keen Guide and Brownie if I hadn't received so much encouragement from Mum. Once I was on my Guiding journey then I had no wish to stop, and here I am, as I write this snippet in 2020, to bring my journey up to date, still having loads of Guiding fun, having now been a member for 70+ years.

Mum had often told me about her Guiding experiences but I didn't ask enough questions. The only tangible evidence I have now is a copy of her record of service, which is minimal. I guess her involvement was more than would seem by reading this. I was fortunate to be able to obtain Mum's record from CHQ in 2009. Sadly, I shall know no more.

I have a record for a Miss Annie Dorothy Hilda Warburton of 101 Tewson Road, Plumstead, SE18 and later of 112 Eglington Road Plumstead:

16 July 1929 - 1931 Lieutenant of 6th Woolwich Company
16 July 1929 - 1930 Brown Owl of 11th Plumstead Girls Friendly Society (St John's Church) Brownies

This is the only record I have for Miss Warburton, she does not appear to have been involved with guiding since 1930.

Letter received from Karen Taylor, Girlguiding Archivist

And so the Guiding tradition in our family continues

Karyn and I propping up B-P's Commemorative stone on Brownsea Island in 1986

Abiee's first introduction to Foxlease was as a baby, still in her pram, at a Foxlease Singing Circle weekend.

Here she is a little older but not yet ready for official membership

Now old enough to make her Promise as a Rainbow
8th November 2001

and as a Brownie in April 2004

Abiee made her Promise as a Guide in Westminster Abbey in February 2007. This was a very special moment for me as, with permission from her leader, Abiee made her Promise to me. Anne (Region Chief Commissioner LaSER) and Angela, (County Commissioner Sussex West) were part of the ceremony. Louisa and her Brownie friend, Kez, and Laura, Abiee's Guide friend, were there too.

Another special moment for Abiee and I was when she renewed her Promise to me as a Ranger outside 'Our Chalet'.

A very proud Louisa just after she made her
Promise as a Rainbow
July 2004

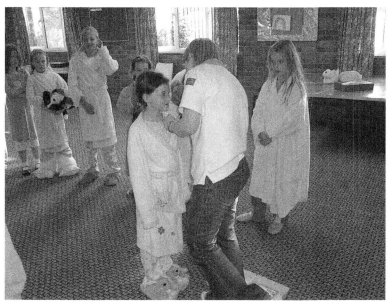

Louisa at her Pyjama Party Brownie Promise Ceremony in 2006

Louisa on Girlguiding Hayling's Carnival Float 2008

Abiee roller bladed her way round the Carnival route
instead of choosing the easy option on the float

A visit to Pizza Hut for Abiee after another Thinking Day Service in Westminster Abbey February 2009

Thinking Day 2010 Westminster Abbey before our presentation of 'Reflections'. Louisa is holding the special "Centenary Duck'

Karyn and Louisa watching the big screen in the Abbey

'Whew, our presentation went well',
said the girls.

Abiee receiving her Baden Powell Award
and, a few years later -

Jacqui (CC) presents Abiee with her Queen's Guide Award.

Abiee is now working with Rainbows, Brownies and Guides in Reading. She was a Girlguidng Advocate until her term of office came to an end. She continues to be a Peer Educator and is now working on her Trainer Qualification.

She contributed the following blog to Huff Post in 2016.

New Research Shows Guides Have Better Mental Health In Later Life - As A Girlguiding Member, I'm Not Surprised!
15/11/2016 12:09

Abiee Harris
20, Girlguiding Advocate and Peer Educator from Portsmouth. Currently studying psychology at the University of Kent.

I have been a member of Girlguiding my whole life and was going to weekly Rainbow meetings before I was even born (my Mum was a leader). Twenty years later it's still something I spend a lot of my time doing - I absolutely love it!
Therefore, I wasn't surprised at all by new research out this week showing that being a member of Girlguiding or the Scouts lowers the risk of mental illness later in life.

The research by the Universities of Edinburgh and Glasgow revealed that taking part in activities designed to develop self-reliance, teamwork and self-learning - all of which I have experienced through Girlguiding - are likely to impact on mental health.

After going to Rainbows, Brownies and Guides when I was younger, I'm now a Rainbow leader and spend an hour a week with a bunch of truly inspiring five to seven year olds. I never leave a meeting feeling down and can always rely on the girls to put a smile on my face.

This isn't all I do though. Throughout my time in Girlguiding, I have done everything from stargazing and climbing mountains to volunteering abroad and travelling to Dubai.

I remember having the chance to plan the theme for an evening meeting as a seven year old Brownie. It made me feel so important and realise that I can have a say and make a difference. Later on, as a Guide, I sang in a talent show. I was terrified. I now sing every week, and was even in the BBC Proms this summer. It can still be scary but I have learnt to put those nerves aside and have confidence in myself.

I think one of the best opportunities I've had through guiding is training to become a Peer Educator. Girlguiding Peer Educators are young women who help Brownies,

Guides and Senior Section members explore important topics such as body confidence and healthy relationships.

We recently launched a new Peer Education programme on mental health called Think Resilient. The new resource helps girls understand what resilience means and encourages them to celebrate their strengths and achievements.
The safe, girl only space provided by Girlguiding really helps girls find their thoughts and feelings and running these sessions has been really beneficial for me too.

As a Peer Educator, I have gained so much knowledge and confidence to the point I can now walk into a room full of girls, whether they're Brownies or Guides, and help them realise their potential. Sadly, this is still very much needed as Girlguiding's Girls' Attitudes Survey 2016 revealed 69% of girls aged seven to 21 feel they're not good enough.

I don't want to live in a world where this is how girls feel. We need to recognise that the point when girls don't feel good enough is the point we need to do something.

I'm proud that I'm contributing to this through my role as a Rainbow Leader and Peer Educator. Each week, I'm helping to provide a space for girls to feel important and valued which, according to this new research, can help reduce their chances of developing anxiety and mood disorders later in life.

I've spent a lot of time talking about what I've done in Girlguiding, but when I think about it, it's these things which have made me who I am today. It's these things which have made me more resilient, more empowered to speak out and most importantly, happy.

Abiee at a Gay Pride Parade with Girlguiding

Louisa renewing her Promise as a Ranger at Pax Lodge in 2014

Louisa taking part in the 'Pinning Ceremony' at PaxLodge

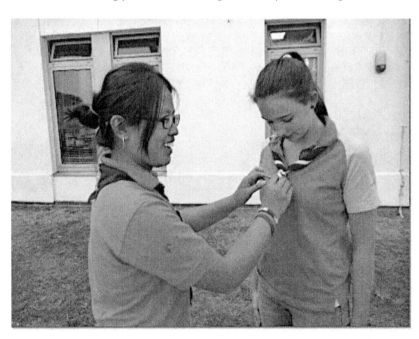

Louisa has now visited two World Centres

Karyn and I taking part in the 'Pinning Ceremony' at Pax Lodge

Swiss Adventures

Karyn celebrated her 18th birthday whilst in Switzerland with Graffham Guides. We were staying in view of 'Our Chalet'.

Karyn on her way to 'Our Chalet' on February 22nd 1997.
We arrived to find the Chalet open but not a soul to be seen to celebrate with.

Switzerland with Graffham Guides
1999

Karyn, Abiee, Louisa and I visited Switzerland and 'Our Chalet' at the beginning of
August 2011

On the steps - where else do you have a photo taken at 'Our Chalet'?

Abiee with her Ranger Promise Badge

Sitting outside the Woodcarver's

With the Woodcarver and his family.

We were made so welcome, as always.

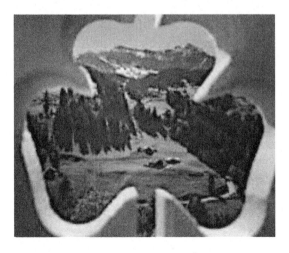

Eunice and I visited 'Our Chalet' in 2018

Almost up to date !!

In March 2019, I took on a new role of County PR so I can't complete my 'Guiding Story' before I've included some PR photos, can I?

Eunice and I are with Alan Mac, MP for Havant.

at Farlington

and in Fareham High Street

Something new for the County was e-news, circulated to Trefoil and Girlguidng members, local MPs, Councillors and supporters. Below is the beginning of our final edition for 2019. Producing this was a steep learning curve but 'I've started – so I'll just have to finish' – to quote the Mastermind Quizmaster.

Welcome to Hampshire East Trefoil e-news three

Wishing all our
members, friends
and supporters
a very
Happy Christmas

Just a few more photos to finish

Joint winners of
'The Bunting Challenge' 2019

Receiving my Silver Voyage Award

and finally

Guiding is about having fun and here I am with Sheila, having the time of our lives, 'playing' on the Merry-Go-Round at Fontwell Racecourse in 2010

The Guide Promise

I promise that I will do my best:
To be true to myself and develop my beliefs,

To serve the Queen and my community,
To help other people and
To keep the Guide Law.

The Guide Law

1. A Guide is honest, reliable and can be trusted.

2. A Guide is helpful and uses her time and abilities wisely.

3. A Guide faces challenge and learns from her experiences.

4. A Guide is a good friend and a sister to all Guides.

5. A Guide is polite and considerate.

6. A Guide respects all living things and takes care of the world around her.

This is why I'm in the Trefoil
Tune: Jumped without a parachute!

I went along to Brownies just to help them out one day.
I must have done a decent job as I was asked to stay.
I really didn't have the time to do the job just right,
But the Guiders all assured me that it only took one night!

Chorus:
This is why I was a Guider (x3)
'Cos the Guiders all assured me that it only took one night.

The District meeting came along and I was asked to go.
It's sad to say the treas-ur-er was ill and didn't show.
So I was asked to do the job and I replied, 'I might',
'Cos the Guiders all assured me that it only took one night!
Chorus:

One day a new Commiss'ner saw me putting up a tent.
She said with great relief to me, 'My dear, you're heaven sent.
I need a Camp Adviser and I know your time is tight,
But I really do assure you that it only takes one night!
Chorus:

The staff at County came to ask if I would give a hand,
To help to plan the AGM and organize a band. I said I really couldn't and I put up quite a fight,
But then they went and told me that it only took one night!
Chorus:

I'd been so long in uniform, my blood was navy blue.
My friends and fam'ly thought me mad, and maybe so do you.
But I'm so proud and happy I'd complain with all my might
If the many jobs in Guiding really only took one night!
Chorus:

So now I'm in the Trefoil Guild and changed the blue to red.
I had to reassure my friends I wasn't 'off my head'.
But being in the Trefoil Guild is really only right,
And I'm still assured the 'Trefoil' things will only take one night!
Final Chorus:
This is why I'm in the Trefoil (x3)
'Cos other members tell me that it only takes one night!

Guiding is about having fun

whether you are a Rainbow

Rainbows from Horndean enjoying themselves lying on the glass floor of the
Spinnaker Tower during the Centenary Celebrations

or a
Trefoil member

with my Sussex West friends, Margaret and Marion

Having fun on Chichester Canal on a grey and dismal day

– but we were far from being dismal, though almost certainly grey!!

July 2011

Acknowledgements

My thanks go to:

my good friend

Margaret Goodyer

County Archivist – Sussex West
For her patience and help with test syllabuses from those early days and for
reading my script.

Karen Stapley

Archivist, CHQ

and, of course, to

Ron

my dear Husband

for all his

support and understanding

of my

Guiding Life and Activities

Trefoil Guild

Appendix

The Brownie Golden Badge Test
(circa 1950)
Brownies needed to pass this to be 'enrolled',
or in today's terminology, 'make their Promise'

For this test you have to understand:

The Brownie Promise

I promise to do my best:

To do my duty to God and the King;
To help other people everyday,
Especially those at home.

The Law

A Brownie gives in to the older folk.
A Brownie does not give in to herself.

The Motto

Lend a Hand

The Salute

The Smile

The Good Turn

The Brownie and Pow-wow Ring

You have to know how to:

Fold and tie your own tie

Plait

Wash up the tea things

The Brownie Golden Bar Test
(I knew this as the Brownie Second class Test)

1. Know how the Union Jack and the flag of your own country are made up and the right way to fly them.

2. Tie the following knots and know their uses: reef, sheetbend, round turn and two half hitches.

3. Show that you understand the rules of the road, and take Brown Owl or Tawny Owl for a 'Stop, Look and Listen' walk.

4. Observe and describe something belonging to the outside world, chosen by yourself, eg sky, sea, bird, tree, flower, animal etc   or
Make a collection of six flowers or shells or feathers etc and name them.

5. Make a useful article to include a turned-down hem sewn with a decorative tacking stitch   or
Darn an article or do the darning stitch.

6. Show two methods of sewing on buttons and sew one button on to a garment.

7. Know how and why you should keep your teeth clean, your nails cut and clean, and why breathe through your nose.

8. Pass two of the following clauses:

    a) From a cross-legged position with arms folded, stand up and sit down in a good style three times.
    b) Without touching the ground with hands or feet, cover a distance of 10 yards on two inverted flower pots or tins.
    c) Balancing a ball on a board about 8 inches square held flat on the palm of the hand, walk with good posture round a figure of eight. Repeat using the other hand.

9. Skip twenty times without a break, turning the rope backwards.

10. Throw a ball against a wall from a point 10 feet away and catch it four times.

11. Lay a table for two for dinner.

The Brownie Golden Hand Test
(I knew this as the Brownie First class Test)

1. Know the alphabet in semaphore; send and read three letters out of four correctly; send and read simple words.

2. Know and understand the meaning of the first and last verses of 'God Save the King'.

3. Set a compass and know eight points.

4. Have taken care of a plant, from seed or bulb and describe to the tester something about the way it has grown, and how it was looked after.

5. Using any slip knot, tie up and address a parcel for the post.

6. Knit a child's scarf or jumper or some other garment.

7. Lay and light a fire. If is it impossible for you to do this, you may be allowed instead to wash and iron a Brownie tie.

8. Cook one of the following: a pudding, a vegetable porridge; small cakes; or equivalent; or prepare a mixed salad.

9. Make tea.

10. Fold clothes neatly.

11. Throw a ball overarm to land over a line 10 yards away within two side lines 3 yards apart.

12. Skip thirty times without a break, turning the rope backwards, and skip any two fancy steps such as: feet crossing; pointing toes forward; turning rope quickly (pepper). *I knew this as 'the bumps'*; hopping with knee raising.

13. Carry a message of at least twelve words in your head for over five minutes and deliver it correctly.

14. Clean and bind up a cut finger and grazed knee.

15. Know what to do if clothing catches fire.

16. Clean shoes.

The Guide Promise (c 1953)

I promise on my honour that I will do my best:

To do my duty to God and the Queen.
To help other people at all times and
To obey the Guide Law.

The Motto

Be Prepared

The Guide Law

1. A Guide's honour is to be trusted

2. A Guide is loyal

3. A Guide's duty is to be useful and to help others

4. A Guide is a friend to all and a sister to every other Guide

5. A Guide is courteous

6. A Guide is a friend to animals

7. A Guide obeys orders

8. A Guide smiles and sings under all difficulties

9. A Guide is thrifty

10. A Guide is pure in thought, word and deed

Guide Whistle and Hand Signals

One short blast	Attention
One long blast	Stop and listen
Succession of short blasts	Fall in
Three short blasts and one long blast	Leaders come here
Succession on long, slow blasts	Extend – go right out
Succession of short and long blasts	Warning – look out

Guide Taps

Day is done, gone the sun,
From the sea, from the hills, from the sky.
All is well, safely rest.
God is nigh

The Guide Tenderfoot Test

1.   Attend Guide meetings for at least a month

2.   Know the threefold Promise, the Guide Law, and the Motto

3.   Understand the meaning of the Good Turn, the Guide Salute,
     Sign and Handshake

4.   Know the whistle and hand signals

5.   Know the composition of the Union Jack, and the flag of your own
     country, the right way to fly them, some of the stories and legends
     connected with them

6.   Whip the end of a rope, tie a reef knot, double overhand, and a round
     turn and two half hitches

7.   Strip and make a bed

8.   Before being enrolled, the recruit should be told something of the origin
     of the Guide movement and the meaning of the Guide and World Badges

The Guide Second Class Test

i.   Intelligence:
1. Have passed the 'Tenderfoot Test
2. Receive and answer a message in Morse across a reasonable distance out of talking range
3. Recognise 12 living things in their natural surroundings, to include any of the following; animals, birds, fish, insects, reptiles, trees, plants or constellations. Discover by observation something of interest about each   *or*
Contribute six interesting notes made from personal observations to a Patrol Nature Log Book   *or*
Keep an individual Nature Log Book containing at least fifteen interesting entries from personal observations   *or*
Stay alone for half an hour in the open and afterwards report on anything seen or heard or smelt
4. Be able to stalk and track

ii.   Handicraft:
Be able to square lash and show practical use of the following knots: reef, sheet-bend, clove-hitch, timber hitch, bowline, sheepshank, fisherman's, round turn and two half hitches, packer's knot
Make a fire out of doors, using not more than 2 matches, and cook on it

iii.   Health
1. Know how to keep healthy and show what you are doing to keep the Rules of Health
2. Cover a mile at Scout's Pace in 12 minutes (30 seconds error allowed each way)

iv.   Service:
1. Treat simple cuts, burns, fainting and choking, and stop bleeding(with pad and bandage on the wound only); know simple treatment of shock, apply a large arm sling and bandage a sprained ankle
2. Make a Morse Signalling Flag (24" x 24") or alternatively make some other article useful to others
3. Strip and make a bed properly, and put your knowledge into practice at home
4. Be able to telephone and know local bus routes

The First Class Test

Throughout the test, the candidate's appearance, carriage, courtesy and common sense are to be taken into account

1. a) Have passed the Second Class Test
    b) Show that you are growing in understanding and practice of the Promise and Law, and has had a good influence in the company.

2. Have camped at least a week-end in a guide Camp. (If this is not possible the Commissioner or Camp Adviser may give permission for the Guide to sleep in a hut).

3. a) Read 'Scouting for Boys' (Boy's Edition) or 'The Wolf that Never Sleeps', or another life of Baden -Powell.
    b) Prove her knowledge of the origin and history of the Guide Movement, including the international aspect.
    Notr: This may be done in a way chosen by the candidate and approved by the Commissioner, such as compiling a book or giving a talk.

4. Understand the meaning of thrift and show you have endeavoured to prevent waste in six practical ways: three with regard to your own property and three with regard to that of other people.

5. Cook Test
    a) Cook and serve, unaided a two-course dinner for a small number (indoors or put as chosen by you)
    b) Answer simple questions to show an understanding of a balanced menu.
    Alternative: Hold the Cook Badge

6. Needlewoman Test
    Make a simple garment, darn a stocking and patch a worn article.
    Alternative: Hold the Needlewoman Badge

7. Child Care Test
    a) Make at the test a timetable for the routine of a child for a day in summer or winter
    b) Keep a child or group of children aged 3 to 5 years happily occupied for one hour

    Alternative: Hold the Child Nurse Badge

8. Go on foot for an expedition of not less than 6 miles

9. Know the rules of Health and prove that you are trying to keep them

10. Swim 50 yards

11. Throw a rope accurately three times out of four
    a) Over a beam or branch approximately three times the height of you.
    b) Within easy reach of a person 12 yards away

12. Have an intimate knowledge of the neighbourhood within a radius of half a mile (town) or one mile (country) of her home or Guide HW. Direct a stranger to the nearest doctor, telephone, pillar box, post and/or telegraph office, Garage and /or petrol filling station, fire, ambulance, police and railway stations etc; give approximate time needed to reach each place. At the test draw a rough sketch map showing the way and the distance from one given point to another. Know to what places the main roads lead.

13. Use a compass and find points by the sun and stars. Read a map.

14. Take two Guides (not First Class) for a half day hike, when possible following a map. Note: The Tester may accompany or join you at any point. You are to be judged on general turnout, programme, organization, manners, care of other people's property, clearing up, enjoyment, type of food and method of cooking.

15. Be prepared to: treat for shock following an accident, arrest bleeding, treat a patient unconscious from accident, fit or fainting, resuscitate the apparently drowned, using the Holgar Nielson method of artificial respiration. Know how to deal with fire, ice and electrical accidents.

16. Change the sheets of a bed with the patient in it. Show how to prevent bed sores and make an ill or old person comfortable in bed. Use a clinical thermometer. Dress a wound.

My Favourite Guide Game

Hats and No Hats

Rules: 2 teams – 'hats' or 'no hats' (or bands and no bands) + bean bag

The game begins with a 'throw up' between team captains. The winning captain secures possession for her side.

The bean bag is thrown between the side in possession whilst trying to get opposing team members 'out' by touching them with the bean bag.

Players must not move when holding the bean bag and they must be holding the bean bag when trying to get opposing members out – ie. Players must not throw the bag at opposing team members to get them out.

If the bag is dropped, the opposing side gains possession.

Should a member of the side that dropped the bag pick it up, they are out as the bag has made contact with them when they are no longer in possession.

The side with no members left in play gains victory.

Alternative rule: (for all members to play all the time, rather than sit out). When out, the 'hats' become 'no hats' or visa versa.

Ordinary Sea Ranger Test

1. Know the history of the ship after which the crew is named.

2. Semaphore: signal and read letters and words.

3. a) Know sixteen points of the compass.
   b) Take a simple bearing.

4. Pipe the 'Still', 'carry on', Pipe the Side'.

5. a) Know the times of the different watches.
   b) Strike ship's time on the bell.

6. Identify the White, Blue and Red Ensigns, and know who are entitled to fly them.

7. Read a nautical book illustrating customs and traditions of the sea.

8. a) Identify four types of pulling boat
   b) Identify in practice the various parts of a boat and of an oar.

9. a) Use six of the following bends and hitches:
      Round turn and two half hitches, bowline, rolling hitch, double sheetbend, bowline on a bight, fisherman's (or anchor) bend, running bowline, packer's knot, timber hitch, highwayman's hitch.
   b) Make a short, back and eye splice
   c) Know eight fancy knots and sennits, including a Turk's Head make a lanyard showing not less than four of these knots.

The Ranger Campcraft Certificate

Qualifications:

Have camped under canvas for at least two weekends as a Cadet or Ranger.

For a Ranger, one of these must have been a mobile or lightweight camp.

Tests:

1. Be responsible for pitching and striking a tent. Know how to care for it in fine and wet weather and carry out small repairs. Erect suitable screening and have a knowledge of camp sanitation.

2. Show a knowledge of cooking out of doors and know how to store food.

3. Know the precautions to take when lighting a fire in any surroundings and how to deal with an outbreak of fire. Identify six different kinds of tree and know their respective value as firewood. Use an axe.

4. Be able to render first aid in an emergency.

5. Draw up a list of personal camp kit. Prove your ability to keep bedding and clothing aired and free from damp.

6. Improvise: one useful camp gadget without string or nails; one using square or diagonal lashing

The Guide Guider's Warrant

1. Qualifications

a) Captain: have attained the age of 21 years
   Lieutenant: have attained the age of 18 years

b) Pass practically the Tenderfoot and Second Class Tests and show that she has an understanding of their educational value.

Have trained he company for at least three months

Show that she understands the importance of co-operation between the company and the pack and follow through to Rangers and Cadets

c) The Commissioner should satisfy herself, by personal interview and, if so desired, a written paper:

That the Guide Guider has a full appreciation of the principles underlying the scheme of training.

That she has some knowledge of the world-wide aspect of the movement both within the British Commonwealth and in other countries, and can apply it to her company.

That she understands the importance in the Guide programme and accepts responsibility for ensuring that her Guides receive this training.

d) The Commissioner should satisfy herself by a visit or visits to the company:

That the right use is being made of the Patrol in council and Court of honour and that the Captain is holding regular training for her Patrol Leaders. Lieutenants must have had experience in assisting with such trainings.

That she can teach some part of the test work to her Patrol Leaders.

That she has the ability to run the whole meeting in a balanced and satisfactory manner.
That she has read and is applying the principles of 'Scouting for boys'.

That she has kept, or been responsible for keeping satisfactory company accounts.

e) A Captain must know the facilities in her neighbourhood for outdoor training and prove that she is using them. She must be able to find a suitable meeting place.

Petworth Reflections

I'm sure you all know why we are here and you don't really need me to tell you – but I will – just incase there's someone in front of me who's very new to Guiding and really not sure.

Firstly, we're here for **Thinking Day** – when we think of our sister Guides throughout the World and ------ the other **really** special celebration is for 100years of Guiding - our **Centenary**.

I was with you at Lodge Hill last September when our celebrations began – wow – what a wonderful day that was.

How many of you were there? I expect you were really tired at the end of the day weren't you – but I bet you had fun! I know I did.

100 years is a **very** long time & it's difficult, isn't it, to really think about that length of time. Where are all you Rainbows and Brownies? Well, your Gt. Gt. Grandmas could have been those very first Guides. That's your Grandma or Nanna's mum. Just think about that.

For you Guides – it may have been your Gt. Grandmas and for all you Leaders – your Grandmas.

For dinosaurs like me, it would have been our mothers who might have been those first Guides. I know that my Mum had been a Guide and a Guider and I wished I had asked her more about Guiding in her time.

If you know anyone older than you who was a Guide, do ask them what it was like in their time – it's so important to keep those memories alive.

So, here we are in this lovely church to celebrate 100 years of Guiding. I can remember being here, in this very same church, to celebrate 75 years of Guiding. My daughter was here too, as a Young Leader, and now she is an adult member with daughters of her own – both of them Guides.

So Guiding just goes from strength to strength.

Now – I want you all to think of the most enjoyable thing you have done so far as a Rainbow, Brownie, Guide, Young Leader, Ranger or Guider.

Have you thought of something yet?

Now, swap your memory with the person sitting next to you.

I expect some of you thought about camping or holidays – yes?

Making new friends or doing new things?

We all have so much fun being a Guide don't we?

Now, you all know that, to become a Rainbow, or Brownie or Guide, we all have to make a promise – our Guide Promise.

I first made my Promise as a Brownie ---- 60 years ago – wow – that's a long time ago isn't it! I've been a member ever since and Guiding has become such an important part of my life – so I hope it is for you too.

When you first make your Promise you are given your Promise Badge, aren't you – different colours for each section. Mine now is a red one as I'm a member of the Trefoil Guild.

Now – I want you to look at the Promise Badge of the person sitting next to you – probably easier than looking at your own.

Look at the colour of it and the shape that's in the circle.

That shape is called a trefoil and it has 3 leaves or petals.

So, when you look at those 3 leaves, it will remind you that your Promise has 3 parts to it.

If you are a Brownie, Guide, Senior Section member or an adult, you promise to do your best to:

One:	love my God
Two:	serve the Queen and my Country
Three:	to keep the Guide or Brownie Guide Law

The Rainbow Promise has 3 parts too:

One:	love my God
Two:	be kind
Three:	be helpful.

The words of the Promise have changed since Guiding began 100years ago but the meaning has remained just the same.

When I first made my Promise, I promised to do my duty to God and the King – as King George V1 was still alive. By the time I had become a Guide, King George had died and Elizabeth had become our Queen.

Maybe, at one of your unit meetings, you could look at the words of the Promise and see how they have changed in those 100 years.

So – 3 leaves or petals on our badge to remind us of the 3 parts of the Promise.

I'm sure you are all able to spell really well. Just think to yourselves for a minute how you spell the word BADGE.

Got it ?   **B   A   D   G   E**

Let's look at the first letter   **B**

B

B could stand for **b**est

When you make your Promise, you promise to do your **best** don't you.

So, I'm sure that you always do your best when you are at your unit meetings and are wearing your Guide clothes but I wonder if you forget sometimes when you're not doing 'Guidey' things.

Maybe you've made something at school and you've rushed to finish it – not bothering to make sure that it was good to look at from all angles – not just the bits that could be seen.

Or maybe you've been helping at home and rushed a job so that you can get out to play - so that whatever you were doing to help your Mum wasn't done properly.

It would be wonderful if, from now on, we all showed everyone what it means to be a Guide by trying to do our very best at all times – whether or not we, or whatever we are doing, can be seen.

I'm so pleased that BP – our Founder – asked us to Promise to 'do our best' & not 'be the best'. If we had to always be the best, I know that I would have failed to live up to the ideals of Guiding many times over. But to 'do our best' is achievable.

So – **B** is for **b**est
A

The next letter is A – now what could that be for?

Well I'm going to say - **A** for **a**ction

We all have so many things to do, don't we and we sometimes put off doing things because we don't feel like it - and sometimes, even important things get forgotten.

I wonder how many times your Guider has asked you to take something the following week to your unit meeting and you have forgotten or left it to someone to take instead.

Maybe your teacher at school has asked you to do something and sadly, you've not bothered.

Even we adults can leave things to others when it should be us doing things.

So let's **show** everyone just what it means to be a Guide.

Let's try to take **action** straight away by doing things when they should be done.

And let's not leave other people to do the things that **we** should be doing.

So – **A** is for action.

Do you remember what the B reminds us?   BEST

<u>D</u>

So – on to the next letter.

D for **d**ifference

Through Guiding we have so many opportunities – to try new things, learn new things, to undertake special projects and to have adventures.

If we take part in all that's on offer to us, through Guiding, it will certainly make a difference to our lives and to the lives of other people too.

So what kind of difference does Guiding make to us:

For a start – Guiding helps us to become independent and confident so that we can do things on our own.

It helps us to face challenges positively and learn from the experience - and that has to make a difference to our lives.

It encourages us to care for other people and to think of others before ourselves.

Now, you **all** know that, as Guides:

> We must try to be honest and reliable, trustworthy & helpful.
>
> We must try to use our time and abilities wisely.
>
> We must also try to always be polite and considerate.
>
> And we must to show respect for all living things and the world around us.

These are very simple rules and should be easy to follow. They are written down as our Guide Law –which we promise to keep and that should help us remember how we should act as a Guide.

If we do our best to do all these things then that will show everyone around us that being a Guide really is making a difference to how we lead our lives - and in turn, will make such a difference to all the people we have contact with – such as our parents and family members, our friends and colleagues at work.

So – **D** is for difference

Let's have a recap:

B is for ?   Best – doing our best

A is for ?   Action – doing things straight away and remembering to do them

D is for?   Difference – making a difference to our lives and those of other people

We're doing well with our spelling !!

What's the next letter in the word 'badge'?

<u>G</u>

G is for **g**iving

Give as much time as you can to Guiding and you will get so much more back.

Probably, if you are a Rainbow or Brownie, that's difficult to understand because you can't see really see what you get back.

But just think of all those friends you have in your unit, all those things you do and have learned, all those opportunities you are given – like sleepovers, Brownie or Guide holidays.

For you older ones – the opportunities are endless: there's the chance to go abroad for holidays, or to work in a voluntary capacity – giving service to others and so much more.

Again, for you older ones – your CV will be much more impressive if your future employers can see that you have **given** time to Guiding. It gives you that 'edge' when applying for higher education or a particular job.

You gain skills and confidence through our Guiding programme. But – you have to **give** in order to **gain**.

So – **G** is for 'giving'

And , here we are at the last letter already:

E

E for - well I can think of 2 things:

E for **e**nthusiastic   and

E for **e**njoy

Be enthusiastic about your Guiding – share your Guiding with your friends – let them see how good it is –

and - above all:

ENJOY your Guiding.

~~~~~~~~~~~~~~~~~~~~~~~~

So – we're here to give thanks for 100 years of Guiding and to remember our sister Guides throughout the World.

Every Guiding member, wherever they may be, will probably have bought, or been given, something to remember this special year.

Maybe you have your special Centenary badge or a pink shirt and spotty necker, like I have.

I've bought something else too and it's in this small tin.

Anyone know what it is?

Yes – it's a flannel – not very big is it?

It reminds me of when Guiding first began all those years ago. There weren't many Guides then and they needed help to get started and grow.

Maybe this flannel needs some help to make it bigger.

Plants need water to help them grow don't they. Flannels also need water to make them work properly – so –

Let's try putting it in water and see what happens.

Wow- it must have grown at least 6 times its size.

And that's just what Guiding is doing – growing. It began with just a handful of girls – probably no more than sitting in this church today - and now we have millions of members all over the world.

So – wear your Promise Badge with pride and show that you belong.

Look at your badge and remember that those 3 leaves or petals of the trefoil signify the 3 parts of our Promise.

Think of the word **BADGE** and remember that:

B stands for	BEST	so do your best at all times
A stands for	ACTION	get stuck in and do things
D stands for	DIFFERENCE	make a difference to yourself and others through your Guiding

G stands for   GIVING give as much as you can to Guiding and you'll gain so much

E stands for   ENTHUSIASM and ENJOYMENT   be enthusiastic and you will enjoy your Guiding so much more.

Let's give 3 cheers for Guiding.

Printed in Great Britain
by Amazon